LISTENING OUTSIDE
LISTENING INSIDE

Ferida Wolff

A *Universal Vision* Book

Universal Vision
P. O. Box 2350
Cherry Hill, NJ 08034

www.feridawolff.com

Cover Art by John Stephens
Cover Design by Nina Sciacca

Library of Congress Catalog Card Number 99-93895

ISBN 0967154-0-6

Printed in the United States of America

First Edition

For Sandra Brossman Bezar,
my dear friend and companion gatekeeper
as well as an extraordinary listener

Acknowledgements

All the stories in this book are about real people who have graciously allowed me to use their names and, by extension, their energies.

I thank every one of you.

CONTENTS

PREFACE

This is not a book. It is an invitation. There is no dress requirement, no RSVP number. Time and date are optional and there is only one guest – you. It is an invitation to listen to your higher self, to connect with the Universe.

Within these pages are stories that have prompted my own listening. Some come from my experiences, some from friends, from teachers, from everywhere and nowhere. They are stories about listening to the inner messages we receive from the Universe and recognizing their outer reflections. They are told from a personal perspective because that is all I can really know. But though a story is about one person, it does not mean that we can't all partake in the understanding. We share myths cross-culturally and have a common humanity. We are, after all, one in the universal sense. It is that connection listening taps into. It is not listening with the ears, although that is often how the deeper listening begins. It is a listening beyond our thoughts, bypassing our egos, tuned into the stillness – a process to which we all have access.

I learned how to listen over the course of twenty-five years as both Yoga student and teacher. Yoga is based on listening – to the breath, to the body, to the mind, and to the spirit. All of these speak to us, if we choose to hear them. I also practice Qi Gong, a Chinese healing art that strengthens and directs the life force. I hold certificates in Foot Reflexology and in Holistic Studies. I have been initiated into first degree Reiki, use Acupressure and Therapeutic Touch. I study Kabbalah (the Jewish mystical system), work with Ayurveda (the Hindu Science of Life based on constitutional types), and do Tai Chi. I am involved with the meditative discipline of Chinese brush painting.

While it may seem like I am doing many things, I am really only doing one thing – deepening my connection with the Universe. When I do one practice, all of them benefit. When I do any of them, all of *me* benefits.

I tell my stories in Yoga classes and workshops and they are there in my writing lectures. We all have stories that have profound meaning for our lives. They are our personal parables, a bridge to the expanded part of ourselves. But we needn't only seek the big stories to feel connected with our higher selves; universal information comes in all sizes and in varying complexities. Myth has it that Isaac Newton was enlightened by an apple that fell on his head. Many a Zen student was awakened by the rap of the master's stick.

Yet, as simple and natural an activity as it is, we would be making a mistake to think that listening is passive; our alert participation is required. It demands we pay attention, if we are to know ourselves, to progress as humans.

I now invite you to open to that higher connection, to discover the inner resources we all possess, to listen to whom you/we truly are.

PATTERNS

PATTERNS

I became aware of patterns through my interest in patchwork quilts. I wrote articles about quilt styles and interviewed quilters. I cut out squares, triangles and hexagons from my family's outgrown clothing in preparation for constructing my own quilts some day. At the time, I did not realize that I was already patching together life patterns from infancy on.

During this period, I went to Spain and visited the Moorish palace of Alhambra in Granada. It was built in the 13th century, in traditional Islamic style, with the outside plain and the inside beautiful. The exterior structure was of solid, red brick while the interior walls, floors and ceilings were decorated in mosaics of brilliant colors and executed in designs that reminded me of American quilt patterns. It fascinated me that these familiar designs were thousands of miles and centuries away from my own creative roots. Was it possible all people instinctively created patterns? Had the Moors, long ago, sought the same kind of order and symmetry as the early American quilters, the same cohesiveness I was looking for in the present day?

The impression of Alhambra remained with me for years. I felt there was a deeper meaning yet to be uncovered. It came to me when I was sorting through the fabric shapes that had cut out and never used. The textures and colors that had once inspired me seemed flat, the carefully graphed designs lacked vitality. In fact, the whole idea of making quilts no longer appealed to me. I felt somewhat guilty that I had used so much material and effort and now was tossing it away. But my interests had changed and quilting was irrelevant; I had moved on. I wondered in how many other areas of my life I had moved on while keeping the patterns of prior needs intact. I observed that other people expressed their lives through patterns, too, frequently similar to mine but with their own variations, patterns that became as fixed as the ones I created for myself.

I understood, then, that the patterns we construct at one point in our lives, even if they serve us well at that time, become static, stone palaces of the past and, through guilt or loyalty or familiarity, prevent us from exploring our present with spontaneity. I doubted that those patterns could be discarded as easily as I shed my fabrics mainly because they weren't as obvious. There are no neat, geometrical shapes in human patterns to guide us. It would take attention to figure out the designs, to spot regularity in seemingly different situations. Fortunately, patterns are predictable and responses to patterns equally so. I suspected that if I became aware of the automatic or patterned parts of my day, I might be able to detect and de-construct the static aspects of life and truly start to live.

How could I do that?

I could learn to recognize that déjà vu feeling, the sense that I have said or done something before.

When my friends tell me stories I have heard more than once, I could examine what I say or do to prompt the repetition.

I could realize that when I use the words *always* or *never* with someone else, I am really talking about a pattern I have created within myself.

I could listen to the boredom I feel and shake myself loose from habits that have me reliving thoughts and actions, emotions and interactions, because it is easier than producing new ones.

In paying attention, some intricate life patterns came into focus. I found a pattern of inattentiveness that caused chaos in my relationships and a childhood pattern of needing to become ill to allow myself a rest. I saw a pattern of withdrawing from confrontation and another of allowing outside events to control my happiness. I was surprised at how many patterns I had created, how I had been teaching myself about life through patterns of pain. The trick was how to respond to life in unpackaged ways rather than rely on new patterns that could easily become as non-functional as cherished old ones.

In Alhambra, patterns remain magnificent examples of period architecture and art. For us, however, they act as our protective façade, the impenetrable palace walls that hide the great beauty within. We can recover our hidden treasures if we have the courage to remove the bricks.

Getting Run Over By Bicycles

"Be careful crossing the street," said my mother. "Are you listening to me?"

I was listening but I guess it was hard to tell. My body was jiggling up and down, impatient to go. My eyes were anywhere but directed toward my mother's face. I was fiddling with the coins in my pocket, the ones that would bring me the delight of a vanilla fudge ice cream cone with chocolate sprinkles. Besides, I was nine years old and perfectly able to take care of myself.

I ran down the front steps, saw my friends on the other side of the street, and after a quick glance around for cars, charged across. I was promptly run over by a bicycle. I returned to consciousness on the black pavement, lying in a circle of staring, frightened faces. I didn't know what had happened. When one of my friends told me, I cried, not because I was hurt but from the shock of it.

My mother sped from our house, white-faced and calling my name. She helped me up, carefully checking for broken bones. Together we hobbled home. She applied a cool washcloth to my forehead and let me rest in the sunlit living room, on the company sofa. The bruises that were sprouting on my legs would soon turn an ugly purple-green and a lecture was sure to come later but I felt like a hero now. I had been run over and lived!

It was not the last time I would feel both the panic and relief of a narrow escape but it was the first time I was aware that something more was going on besides my ignoring my mother's words and getting instantly caught. I had heard what she said but had I really listened? Did it sink in? Might I have avoided a painful bruising by paying attention?

I had begun listening, although in a backdoor kind of way. Most of my listening was done in hindsight, recognizing, after the fact, that I was being told something. It might have come from a stranger, a friend, a feeling, a voice inside that sounded like mine but knew something I didn't.

I read books, attended workshops, joined organizations. I put myself in situations that could nurture learning but I didn't necessarily learn. The problem was that I did not always receive what I was hearing. If it came into conflict with what I wanted to do, I declared it nonsense. I continued to symbolically throw myself in front of bicycles.

Years later, in the middle of an argument with my husband, I was suddenly aware of the dynamics that were occurring. I was really listening. I had heard all this before. I would try to get him to admit he was wrong and I was right. He would yell louder. I'd get quieter. He would storm, I would fume. No one ever won. He'd feel wronged, while I would carry the hurt and emotional bruises with me which were every bit as painful as that long ago bicycle encounter. It was a familiar pattern. I could continue to do it this way or choose another path.

So instead of a blaming session, I smiled. We each wanted something. We could talk about how we could both win. I avoided being run over. It was a nice change.

As I became aware of more patterns, I was run over by fewer bicycles. It made life a lot easier.

I thought it would be a momentous revelation when I realized I could avoid a collision, but it wasn't. It was as easy as floating downstream instead of swimming against the rushing water.

It was as calming as swinging in a hammock.

As pleasing as a sunrise.

As natural as breathing.

Simple as a smile.

Feeling Free

I woke up feeling cranky. I didn't want to write although a chapter needed editing. I didn't want to do housework, though the laundry was piling up. I didn't want to do anything that resembled responsible behavior. It was that kind of day.

As I drank my morning tea, I thought I felt a headache coming on. Yes, there it was, a dull throb just behind my eyes. Maybe I should go back to bed until it subsided. As I put the dishes in the sink, it seemed that my muscles were beginning to ache. Or was the ache in my joints? That could mean I was coming down with the flu. I absolutely should be in bed.

I wiggled under the covers and shut my eyes. Another couple of hours of sleep would be so nice only I was now completely awake. I ought to get up. But no, there was that headache and the beginning of a sniffle. Better get the tissues.

On my way back from the bathroom with a family-sized tissue box, I stopped to grab that big new novel I had bought but had no time to read. I opened the book and settled against the pillows. Fifty pages later, I had the guilty thought that if I didn't get through editing the chapter today, I would have two chapters to edit tomorrow. I lifted up on my elbows. Was it stuffy in the room or was I getting a fever? I drooped back down.

The morning was moving along and so was my reading. Another twenty pages and I was stretching. It 's about time I got up and did the wash, I thought. But what if I was contagious? I certainly didn't want to spread any germs.

I suddenly had the notion that this thing could last a week, maybe more. That would put a serious crimp in my plans but what could I do, I mean, if I was sick?

Ten pages more and I was getting restless. It would be very inconvenient to be laid up for a week. Maybe I wasn't actually getting the flu. I didn't really want to be sick. To be truthful, all I wanted was a little acceptable time off. I needed to nurture myself away from people, chores, career, the outside world. Did I have to wait to be sick to do that? As a child, the only respite from school or family chores was illness. But I wasn't a child any more. Did I have to manufacture symptoms to provide myself with an excuse? No, I decided, I didn't.

I talked to myself. Okay, I said, you need a day to yourself. Admit it. Accept it. Toss out the guilt and enjoy a mini-vacation. What would you like to do? Read? You're already doing that. Pamper yourself? Take a bubble bath. Be a hermit? Let the machine answer the phone.

Funny how the aches subsided in the heat of the tub. They just slipped away with the last of the bubbles down the drain. My head felt just fine, the throb replaced by a sense of well being.

By late afternoon, I was back typing with enthusiasm, refreshed physically, mentally, and emotionally. And rather than feeling helpless, I felt empowered. I had given myself permission to listen and respond to my needs, to care for myself the way I tended to my family. I didn't need the crutch of illness to justify a rest. It was such a simple awareness but then isn't it the simple things that set us free?

I Just Hate That!

When I was growing up, we used to tell jokes about how stupid we could be. Here's one I remember:

Patient: Doctor, Doctor, can you help me? My foot hurts
          when I jab it with this stick.
Doctor: I can cure you. Throw the stick away and you
          won't have any more pain.
Patient: You're a miracle worker!

The times were simpler then and less graphic. Saturday Night Live updated that old gem years later with more descriptive stupidity that went something like this:

I hate when I stick a pencil in my ear and it comes out the other side and my brains are hanging off the eraser. I just hate that.

Well, I hate when I watch television just before I go to sleep and I see three killings, a few beatings, an explosion or two and a fatal fire and I have terrible dreams and wake up exhausted. I just hate that. And frankly, even though television is supposed to entertain, I don't find the violence at all amusing.

Why do we do things like that to ourselves?

I've decided to take the doctor's advice and cure myself. I am no longer at the tyranny of the stick or in this case, the remote control. I've stopped watching shows that I know will set me up for nightmares.

It has taken me a long time to make that connection. I was in the habit of relaxing before going to bed by watching TV. I saw police dramas, magazine exposés and action movies. I dined on crime, snacked on violence. The eleven o'clock news spoon-fed me more. I felt captive to the tube. I didn't want to, or couldn't, move. So, night after night, I listened and dreamed.

I knew of the studies that showed television viewing alters brain waves from an active to a passive state. It is hypnotic. That's why commercials are so effective; they enter the subconscious mind when it is very receptive.

Did I have to keep poking that pencil in my ear so that advertisers could sell me another pencil? It did not make any more sense that the patient continuing to jab himself in the foot with a stick.

So instead of numbing myself before the television, now I listen to jazz instead. Sometimes I write a letter to a favorite friend. I may choose an uplifting book or magazine to read in bed. My last thoughts are not violent. I relax into sleep, set for a positive dream state.

And I leave the television to the jokesters who say, I hate it when I swim in quicksand and it drags me down and sucks on my eyeballs and when I grab a vine and finally get out, I jump right back in. I just hate that!

Teaching Myself

I am a teacher. I teach myself daily how to be human through my mistakes.

I teach myself when to be quiet and when to speak up by talking at the wrong times and remaining silent when it is appropriate to speak.

I teach myself compassion by turning away someone genuinely in need and then regretting it.

I teach myself about love when I argue with the people I love the most.

I teach myself the value of friendship by alienating a friend because of not listening with an open heart.

I teach myself to be responsible when I see my pet cockatiels scrounging in the food dish I forgot to fill.

I teach myself to seek inner beauty by sometimes fooling myself into thinking nice manners alone make nice people.

I teach myself about pleasure through the pain of withholding joy from my daily life.

I teach myself understanding by getting stuck in the same old patterns time and again.

I teach myself humility when I embarrass myself by showing off.

I teach myself to offer kindness when I refuse it for myself.

I teach myself moderation by overwhelming myself with too many tasks.

I teach myself patience by rushing through life instead of enjoying it.

I teach myself happiness through the frustration of trying to control what is not in my control.

I teach myself peace each time I am disturbed by problems not my own.

I teach myself about myself by pretending to be someone else.

I teach myself about God by feeling the loneliness of depending upon myself.

BOOK REPORTS

BOOK REPORTS

When my English teacher assigned a book report, there were silent groans throughout the classroom; I come from a generation when verbal dissent was not acceptable. Questions, however, were allowed. *How long did the book have to be? How many pages did we have to write?* Our teacher answered the spoken questions but we all knew the sub-text; *How few pages could we get away reading? Is it okay to write big?*

I was the rare kid who liked book reports. Actually, it wasn't the report itself but the reading that was important to me. The assignment gave me permission to do what I wanted to anyway – read. My parents couldn't tell me to do something useful because I already was; I was doing homework. If I had to give my opinion about what I was reading, that was little enough payment.

The mile-and-a-half walk to the Fresh Meadows branch of the public library became my ritual as each week I brought back the four books I was allowed to borrow with my junior card so I could take out another four to occupy the next week. I could have taken the bus or hopped on my bicycle to get there but I never did, at least not to that library. I liked to prolong the anticipation.

That was my exploring library. There I discovered Langston Hughes and Agatha Christie. I ogled the anatomically correct pictures in *Gray's Anatomy.* I brazenly returned to the children's section under the guise of junior high research to reconnect with Dr. Seuss.

There were other libraries in my sphere; New York City was a library heaven. I did ride the bus to the large Jamaica branch to do serious research when I actually had a report to work on. And I frequented the Windsor branch for its collection of young adult fiction where I could indulge my pre-teen fantasies of boys and dates and what the grown-up world promised.

I was an absolutely non-discriminating reader. I read everything and believed everything. If the words were on the page, they must be true. To me, fiction was as true as non-fiction in the sense that it portrayed life as it really was. Even science fiction could be true, how did I know? To doubt was to block the whole-hearted pleasure I received from the written word.

I eventually developed criteria for my reading but it took well into my adult years for that to happen. It also took years for me to realize that as we grow in understanding, the books we are drawn to read change as well. It's as if we graduate from one library section to the next, from the children's section to junior books, from adult readings to scholarly works, and somewhere there is a divine librarian handing us a card for the next level. I have outgrown books in many sections but I am no longer in school, so I don't have to report on them.

And now, free of that constraint, the roles have reversed on me. I am not the one doing the reporting, the books are. They are not only giving me their opinions, they are offering me a vehicle for going deeper into myself. The books I choose to read reflect my needs, my development, my understandings. They are essays on my career and diagram my life's path. They indicate my emotional state and defuse the stress that sometimes threatens to overwhelm me. Romance novels speak as eloquently as Shakespearean sonnets. And children's books continue to delight me.

I have become my own librarian and have given myself the ultimate library card: the freedom to read, or not, as I choose, from the whole glorious, extensive, varied literature of life.

Page Ninety-Nine

I had been reading a book about Kabbalah, Jewish mysticism, for five years. I admit to being a slow reader but I am not *that* slow. I was on page ninety-nine with 533 more pages to go. Some books are like that. They have so much to say that even when you get to the last page, you know that you're still at the beginning.

Each Wednesday, I went to Rabbi Serebryanski's house to study this book. Other people showed up, too, but not always the same people. We sat around the table with our books unopened but we knew we were on page ninety-nine. For two months, the rabbi, who preferred to be called Yossi, had begun the class by saying, "We're on page ninety-nine." Before that, we were on page ninety-seven for six weeks or so. Sometimes we would read one sentence, sometimes a few words. Often, we didn't read at all.

When the class was ready to begin, we all opened our books – to page ninety-nine. Yossi reviewed what we did last week. That frequently sparked a question or a story and we'd be off into a new discussion. Maybe we would read that night, maybe not.

New people came to class with expectations. They came to study the book. As the talk went on, bouncing from one person to another, they often became impatience. They'd say, "Let the rabbi speak." But it was the rabbi's words that started the discussion. They would say, "Can we get back to the book?" We'd laugh and fiddle with the pages but the discussion would continue. Once a newcomer mumbled under his breath that there was no control in the class.

When the time was the right, Yossi would bring us back to page ninety-nine. He brought our discussion back to where we started but somehow it felt as if we were at a different place, that we had worked hard. We were surprised that two hours had passed. The discussion frequently continued as we put on our coats and pretended we were leaving. It would be another hour before everyone said goodnight.

Some new people never came back. Now and then, one would. He would come early the next week and find a comfortable space at the table. When someone would ask, "Where are we?" he would laugh with the rest of us and say, "We're on page ninety-nine."

Underlining Rainbows

I once had an English teacher who held up his copy of Joseph Conrad's *Heart of Darkness,* the book we were going to read that semester. It looked as if he had underlined the pages in rainbows. He told us that no matter how many times he read the book, it spoke to him. So each time he underlined the sentences that jumped out at him, that showed him something he hadn't seen before. Some lines had five or six colors under them. He said he needed to get a new copy because this book was getting hard to read but he would never throw it away. He wanted to see where he had started and where he had come so far. That year he was underlining in purple. I wondered if he would run out of colors before the book stopped talking to him.

Outgrown Ideas

I didn't know I could outgrow a book the way I used to outgrow my jeans. When they became too short, I only wore them inside where no one would see me. When the waist got too snug, I loosened the seams. When they felt too tight to breathe in, I reluctantly put them in a box to give to my younger cousin. Only instead of giving them away, I hid them in back of my closet. Sometime during the year, my mother would find the box and get rid of it. It was okay, though, because I was busy loosening another set of seams.

Years ago a friend said I had to read a great book he found. It would tell me how to live my life. I read it and it did. Think this, it said, and your life will go smoothly. Do that, it said, and you'll be happy. For a while, I thought this and did that and it seemed right.

Then I started reading other books. I talked about the ideas in them. Sometimes, I found new ideas popping into my head, ideas I hadn't read. I talked about those, too. For a while, I stopped thinking this and doing that.

Yesterday, a different friend told me she was reading a book and wanted to know what I thought of it. It was the same book my other friend had recommended. I took it from my bookshelf to re-read but I couldn't get into it. Its ideas were too small. How could I only think *this* when there were so many other ways to think? How could I only do *that* when there was a world of things to do?

I felt as if I couldn't breath in it. I knew why. The book didn't fit me anymore. I put it in a box in back of my closet. Someone, someday, might need a perfectly good, outgrown pair of ideas.

Reading Books

I used to think that if I started reading a book, I had to read it to the end. I don't know why I thought that. I know I read books that I hated and books that left me depressed. I wondered why I wasted my time reading them. Some books I had to read for school or for a job, like it or not. It took me a while to realize that I could choose what to read for myself. Over the years, I developed some informal guidelines about reading. They keep changing, though, as I learn more about what I need from books.

If a book gives me a lift, I'll read it.

If a book depresses me, I won't read it.

If a book speaks to me, I'll read it.

If a book talks down to me, I won't read it.

If I start thinking that this is a book I want to share with a friend, I'll read it.

If a friend recommends a book, I'll begin to read it but I may not finish it.

If a book is on the best-seller list, I may read it and then maybe I won't.

If a book leaves me with ugly images I can't shake, I won't read it.

If a book really gets me involved with the characters, I'll read it.

If a book gives me information I want to know, I'll read it.

If a book helps me understand myself better, I'll read it.

If a book shows me something new about what it means to be human, I'll read it.

RESISTANCE

RESISTANCE

Sometimes, I think I only learn when the lesson is so big I can't possibly ignore it. I don't know why it needs to be this way. It doesn't seem to be an inherited trait. Perhaps it is that society throws so many distractions in the path that no one can completely tune them out. It might be that knowing what is in my highest interest runs counter to what I want so I resist the awareness until it becomes downright unwise to disregard it.

Yet, it isn't that this information is not being received. Subtle messages come in a variety of forms, through everyday experiences. It is that gut feeling that advises caution. It is a slight hesitation before committing to an action. It is getting an answer from the heart before coming up with a more logical one from the brain.

My friends have their own recognizable triggers that signal them to pay attention. Dolores has her red flag alert, a mental response to something that should be examined more closely. Jeannie gets goosebumps when she hears what, for her, is absolute truth. I get chills when I know, intuitively, that something is right. But we occasionally turn away from inner knowledge when it conflicts with our desires. We are human, after all.

And that just might be the problem. While it is important to accept our humanness with its physical, emotional, and mental components, it is equally necessary that we recognize the supra-physical or *the more than what we see is what we get* aspect of our existence. We know more than our components are willing to admit.

Maybe resistance is inherited but in the human genes as a species rather than in individual DNA. The pull of the physical is strong. It takes faith to accept that we are more than the sum of our parts when our physical beings are so immediate, so here. The subtle has a hard time getting heard and when it is, too often, it is labeled imagination and dismissed.

Imagination, intuition and gut feelings are all ways of accessing information. We just are not used to registering them as valid because they come from the softer side of knowing rather than from the logical, show-me part of our minds. If we can get past the need to see things with our physical eyes, then we might benefit from listening to those sources of knowledge that speak gently within us -- before they begin to shout.

The Big Dog

Cindy got herself into a fix. She was invited to be part of an energy circle. The aim of the group was to send energy to people who needed it, an objective she thought to be wonderful. It sounded like something she wanted to participate in and the group seemed to be one in which she would belong.

On the day of the meeting, Cindy was introduced to lots of nice people. The host's house was beautiful. There was Sox, a big, friendly dog, out in the front yard greeting everyone. It all seemed so perfect, except that she felt uneasy. A doubt kept buzzing in her head. She felt it in her stomach. Cindy didn't understand why, but she knew she wasn't meant to be there.

Just as she thought of leaving, the leader instructed the group to hold hands and form a circle. Then she told them that they must not break the circle because it would scatter the powerful energy they were creating. Cindy took the hand of the person to her right. She immediately had the sensation that she wanted to let go. It was equally uncomfortable on the left. She convinced herself that she was being silly and continued to hold hands and feel uncomfortable.

Cindy had trouble keeping her mind on what was happening. She really wanted to leave but was too polite to say anything and she certainly did not want to disturb the energy of the circle. She silently asked the Universe for a sign to tell her what to do. Soon her hands started to feel itchy. Was it a sign? She wished she could scratch but that would mean letting go and breaking the circle. She decided it was only an itch and again asked the Universe for a sign, perhaps a bigger one.

She felt a tingling in her hands this time. Maybe this was the sign. It got so strong, it was as if she was getting little electrical shocks. She wanted desperately to let go but everyone was swaying with the energy and she didn't want to mess things up. Cindy held on as her mind cried out for a sign, a big sign, one she could recognize, one that would tell her clearly what to do.

Just then, Sox got loose and charged into the house, eager to play. He pushed through the circle, breaking Cindy's handhold. Then he went on to disrupt the rest of the group until there was no circle. As the host took him out, hands began to clasp again. Cindy stepped back, out of the circle, and quietly left.

On the way home, she thanked the Universe for sending her the Big Dog.

The Cosmic Kick

I had been a Yoga teacher for about six years when I received the message through meditation that it was time for me to cut back on my teaching. It was a surprise. I liked teaching. Rather than cutting back, I was gearing up for more classes.

I was already teaching at a community college and a local adult school. I was scheduled for two new classes at the college in the fall and had picked up a teaching assignment at another college for the following semester. Cut back? Not now.

My college class began with a problem that spring. We didn't have a regular meeting place. We started out in a dance studio, then were sent to the front of a lecture hall. When that was needed for a program, we did our postures in the lobby of the school theater. We finally ended up in the art gallery. I joked about our learning the concept of flexibility but the situation was less than satisfactory.

My other class was doing fine. But I kept hearing the message, *Are you ready to cut back on your teaching?* I wasn't.

In the fall, my class had an assigned room but there was no appropriate space to hold my new classes. They would have to be postponed until the next semester.

I started teaching and noticed right away that something was different. There wasn't the cohesiveness of my prior classes. All the students were perfectly attentive and seemed to respond well to the practice. One-by-one they told me how much they were enjoying the class but the group feeling that usually coalesced by the third week never happened. It was as if I was tutoring twenty-eight students individually. Rather than sharing and building on a powerful communal experience, we were isolated within the same space.

When the semester ended, I wished everyone well but breathed a sigh. Surely, the spring class would be better. This was just a matter of a strange group dynamic. In my quiet moments, I again heard, *Are you ready to cut back on teaching? You have other work to do.* What other work could it be? I must be making this up.

The spring semester began with the new classes being cancelled because of poor registration. At least I had a group of students for my regular class that seemed more enthusiastic. As the season progressed, however, I found that only half of them showed up at any one time. There was no continuity, no commitment.

My adult school echoed my college class. Nine people registered but only four showed up each week and they were never the same four! I found myself teaching and re-teaching the same postures, never knowing who knew what. In addition, the enrollment in both classes strangely plummeted; the full classes I had been accustomed to were ancient history and the waiting lists evaporated.

What was happening? I was on a ship in distress. *Are you ready to cut back...?* I was bailing frantically but it was still my ship.

The final blow came when I taught my first and only semester at the new college. This group seemed intent on sinking the ship. The energy of the students was so scattered that I had to mentally smooth it out before I entered the room. One student was eager to challenge me on a psychic level. Another hugged me one week, hated me the next. Every session was an exercise in remaining centered. I dreaded each class. Everything I was doing drained my energy.

Are you ready...?

I was ready.

I hadn't listened and had gone through a series of intensifying situations until I couldn't ignore the message. It took me a year-and-a-half to face up to it. When I wouldn't do it myself, the Universe stepped in and gave me a cosmic kick. I finished the semester and resigned all my teaching assignments. I was ready to move on to that other work, whatever it might be.

But the Universe wasn't finished yet. *Are you really listening?* it seemed to say.

I was offered three jobs the week after I stopped teaching. Each one had its appealing aspects. They were all part-time teaching positions so I could do all of them if I chose and still be available for that other work. The Universe knew how to push my buttons.

One of the jobs was Yoga instructor in the gym where I train. I could probably barter my classes for free training sessions.

Another offer was to teach teenage gymnasts. I often dreamed of doing Yoga with kids.

The third job would have me teaching in my own studio, in a brand new carpeted space, where I could make my own hours and run my own show. I used to yearn for such a place.

Were these opportunities or tests? How would I know?

The doubts kept piling up. They had lives of their own and pretty pushy ones at that. They came calling like unwanted guests. I learned long ago that I didn't have to admit visitors whether it was on my doorstep or through my telephone. So why should I usher the doubts inside? I took a deep breath and calmed myself. I knew what I had to do.

Yes, I told them, I understand you would like to visit but I'm afraid I am otherwise occupied. You see, I am going to be very busy soon.

I turned down all the jobs with a polite thank you and a reference for a friend who was very excited – she wanted to do all those things as much as I had. No one was left unattended and I was free to move on to that new work and the next installment of life's adventure.

Therése

My friend, Therése, taught in elementary school. It was a steady job and a career she loved. She lived in a small apartment, filled with lovingly chosen antiques, on a quiet suburban street. She wrote poetry when she had the time and belonged to a group where she nervously read her poems and was surprised when they were praised.

One day, Therése became aware of an inner prompting. She tried to ignore it because it made her think of doing things that made no sense. It made her think of quitting the job she loved so she could write full time. It made her think of selling the antiques she had collected for so many careful years, and leaving her apartment. These were not comfortable thoughts.

But the prompting would not go away. It spoke to her of putting her vision of the world on paper for others to see. It told her to simplify her life so that the only thing she could claim was her vision and her poetry.

I was worried for Therése. Her face was pinched and she curled her shoulders inward to protect herself. Even the long, dark braid that hung lushly down her back seemed frazzled.

"Am I crazy?" she asked her friends and walked away still not knowing.

She called in antique dealers to appraise her furniture. They offered less than she wanted, less than she needed. She couldn't possibly sell her treasures for what they would pay.

During the summers, she traveled and her vision grew. She looked at her beginning poems and found them lacking. They were limited by her limitations. So she sold her furniture. She gave up her job. She did not sign another lease.

She went to the shore to write. She was scared and uncertain. What had she done? What would she do? Her friends did not see her for many months. Out on her own, her whole life changed.

She published a volume of poetry in the spring. She does readings and workshops. She has no steady job and works harder than ever. She house-sits or makes arrangements for places to stay.

When I see Therése, now, I am aware of her confidence. People would never know of her other life if she didn't tell them but she does. It is in her poems, part of her vision.

I watch her walk straight-backed, with a grace that is emphasized by the sweep of her long, black dress. Her brow is at ease. I notice how intently she listens when someone asks her a question, as if the rest of the world has disappeared. Mostly, I am fascinated by her smile, mouth round and eyes wide as a child's. She seems to be always on the edge of the next exciting second.

She no longer asks if she is crazy.

Can You Talk?

The telephone lines are being repaired on my street. This isn't the first time communication has failed but considering the volume of electrical messages that pulse through them, telephones are truly modern miracles.

Yet, no matter how wonderful our technology, we can do better. Humans have natural phone lines, if we would only learn to use them.

We even have built-in answering machines. They give us messages without the inconvenience of having to press a button to listen; the information simply appears in our awareness.

I learned to heed the messages from the ethereal telephone company the painful way, after my friend Harriet had surgery. She came out of it well and was doing fine. She was back home, getting on with her life. We had just spoken two days before I became aware of the message to call her.

"Why?" I thought. "Is she okay?"

I heard inside my head that she was physically well but that her husband had died.

"This is sick," I thought.

Her husband was not ailing. I saw him two weeks before and he was happy, active, vital. Why would I think such a thing. And yet, should I call? How could I say, "I'm calling to find out if your husband is alive?"

So I didn't call. I promised myself I would call next week, just to say hello.

Next week I was busy. And the week after was just as full. We usually spoke every month or so. I would catch up then. When I finally called, two months had passed since I last saw her.

"Did you hear?" she asked.

"Hear what?"

"My husband died."

"I didn't know," I said. "I'm sorry."

"I thought you probably didn't or you would have been at the funeral."

I felt terrible about the situation. I had let her down somehow. But how could I have been there when I didn't know? It took me a few days to realize what had happened.

Yes, I would have been at the funeral. I would have commiserated with her friends and family. I would have offered her the love and support she needed from me at the time. It was too late to do any of that because I hadn't used the modern instrument to verify what I had learned through the ancient one; I hadn't answered the cosmic phone call.

I called Harriet and confessed that I really did know about her husband but I hadn't trusted enough in my intuition to act on the message I received. It was a hard confession. I had let both of us down. I didn't know how that would affect our friendship.

She was the one who commiserated with me. She comforted me in my grief and supported my growing intuitive confidence. Our friendship became more solid and intimate.

It is rare that two weeks pass, now, without a call. We have so much to say to each other on the many levels that have opened up between us.

The other night I was thinking of her, wondering if it was too late to call because we don't usually speak in the evening. Not one second passed when the phone rang.

"Can you talk? Harriet said.

She was thinking that maybe I was busy, that it was night, that I might not want to talk at that time but she got the message to call. I grinned.

"I can talk," I said. "Can you?"

Madeleine's Poem

Madeleine was in the third grade when I was introduced to her. At eight years old, she sometimes had trouble sitting still. She would rather be dancing or singing, maybe listening to music or watching TV. She enjoyed drawing and making up stories to tell but didn't much like to read. She wasn't fond of writing, either, but when she was in the mood, she could write incredible poems.

One day Madeleine was watching the birds in her backyard. She wasn't doing anything, just listening, she said, and she felt like writing this poem:

The Birds in My Back Yard

Swift, swift
the robin, the hawk, the songs fill my heart
like love fills the soul,
like the wind frees personality,
like hope freezes time,
like heart fills the WORLD!

The day I was in Madeleine's class, she was crying because someone had accused her of taking a book that didn't belong to her. She hadn't; the book was found. It was not the first time tears flowed and I'd be surprised if it were the last. Life can be tough for a listener of any age but especially difficult for one so young. I recognized the distress she was feeling because I, too, had shed many school tears. Yet, I knew that the source of those tears was the source of the poems.

She didn't seem aware that she had written anything special. In fact, she was embarrassed to let me see her poetry. I told her that her poem was good, not to be kind but because it was.

Indeed, I'll look for her name on books in the future. I'll seek out her poems in literary magazines where I know they will be found if she is brave enough to keep listening – and if Madeleine ever decides she likes to write.

NEGATIVE SPACES

NEGATIVE SPACES

I love 3-D books. It is fun to see how the computer-arranged pictures, repeated on the page like tightly patterned wallpaper prints, change from a flat design to one with depth and dimension, suddenly revealing images that were invisible at first glance. It happens in the shift of an eye.

I know how to make the shift to turn the ordinary world into one that is and isn't there. To bring in the hidden image, I gently cross my eyes. After a slight delay while I process the new visual information, the background separates from the foreground and there is a scene that I did not see before. I know it isn't magic but it amazes me all the same.

Artists know of the importance of seeing what isn't there. They call it the negative space. It defines what the viewer sees by outlining the positive shape. The negative space has a presence of its own that appears quietly, in the background. It hates to be pushy so it waits to be noticed. Sometimes, consciously, it isn't noticed because the positive space is so demanding of attention. Yet we could not see the positive without the negative being there. They are partners – one automatically creates the other.

The three dimensional pictures can be teased out of the background by changing visual perspective. To become aware of the negative space of a painting or a thought, to read between the lines or hear what is unspoken, more is required. I find I have to "cross my brain" and allow the left, no-nonsense, logical part of me that sees the positive aspect to relax so that the adventurous, creative right brain can assert itself. It offers its quiet information to anyone willing to hear it.

When I took up Chinese brush painting, my teacher told me to let the brush paint. It wasn't easy to do. My hand wanted to be the guiding force of the stroke. Fortunately, both teacher and brush were patient. It was the same writing Haiku. I wanted control, but only after relinquishing it to be open to the essence of the poetic image was control possible.

Negative spaces come in more than just artistic contexts. Wherever there is a gap, a disconnected-ness, an interruption, there is an opening for observing something hidden, the negative that defines the positive. Intuition is in that opening.

The gap is not a lack. It is a fullness of the hidden, as thin air is filled with gasses, unseen but nonetheless real. There is movement in the interaction between negative and positive spaces that exercises the logical and creative processes and keeps us in balance.

I try to be aware of the gap when I am stuck with a problem.

I say to myself, "This is what I see or think or know. What am I missing?"

If I become still for a few moments, the shift will happen. Expecting it, I am once again amazed – and amused – when it does.

Chinese Brush Painting

Sister Mary Gavin is an artist. She teaches me the traditional art of Chinese brush painting. She shows me how to make the ink by rubbing the black ink stick against the wet, grinding stone until it feels like pudding. She helps me to hold the hollow bamboo brush against the rice paper so that the hairs form a curve and the brush will work for me. She draws each stroke on her own paper so that I can copy it.

I watch her put one stroke next to another. There is a fish. Her hand brings the brush down, barely grazing the paper before it rises once more, like an airplane landing and taking off again. A leaf remains. Rocks form where there is only paper.

I raise my brush in imitation of Mary's technique and apply it to the paper. It makes a clumsy stroke. I do not see a fish or a leaf. If there are rocks anywhere on my paper, they are hiding. I do it again. And again. And again. I know I am trying too hard and expecting too much.

I stop looking for fish and leaves. I am aware only of the brush. My body moves with it, is an extension of it. Calm settles into me as I release the effort of creating. One stroke next to the other. A flower appears.

"Where did that come from?" I ask.

"From the stillness," Mary says.

She smiles.

I notice I am crying.

Ancient Voices

Kata Tjuta is a rock formation in the middle of the Australian outback. The Europeans who discovered it 150 years ago called it the Olgas, naming the red domes for Queen Olga of Germany and ignoring the aboriginal people's 60,000-year claim to its guardianship.

It is a powerful place. The aborigines have used it from ancient times to pass on religious teachings to their people. They say it is too private to share with outsiders. The tourists who visit walk among the stones and listen to the tales the guides tell. That seems to be enough. They would understand more if they walked among the guides and listened to the stones.

I felt Kata Tjuta before I saw it. When I stepped onto the red walkway, I imagined myself to be inside a great beating heart. The walkway was long. It spanned desert sands that led to a shallow pool hidden behind an unexpected cluster of trees. Some children played on the small bridge that arched over a trickle of water while their parents stayed back, snapping pictures for their photograph albums.

I was alone in the heartbeat, midway between the two groups. I sat on the sand and closed my eyes, listening to the echoes of the voices around me. I heard what they were saying although no one was close enough for my ears to pick up their words. Sound was bouncing everywhere. It was impossible to pinpoint the location of any source. It was so loud that at times I covered my ears and wished for the people to be quiet. They eventually moved on and I was left to the tremendous silence of the stones.

It was then that I heard the other voices. They did not echo but spoke clearly within me. I sensed that they were the voices of the ancient ones.

Whatever you do comes back to you.

I looked around for the others. Could they hear that?

Laughter came at me from the right. Shouts assaulted me from the left. No one was listening to the voices of the stones. Only I heard them, as I sat in the silence between the echoes, and wondered what else the stones had to say.

Haiku

I came to poetry late in my literary development. It had been part of the public school curriculum, of course, but was taught in such a way that I never connected it with me as a person. I was a reader memorizing, dissecting, imitating the work of a category of writers known as poets. Without an assignment, there was no reason to read poems.

Then I discovered Haiku. Three tightly regulated lines of intensity. How could so much feeling and association be crammed into that minimal format?

In the Japanese language, the first line consists of five syllables, the second has seven, and the third has five. In English, because voiced syllables are different, the structure is slightly more flexible. Each verse relates to a season and evokes a mood.

At last, here was poetry I could feel. It was so simple, I could write it, easy. I wrote some poems. They had the correct number of syllables and the appropriate subject matter but something was wrong. I used descriptive words but they crowded the poems. I put in emotion, which confused the form. Nothing worked.

I went to the library and took out slim volumes of Haiku. I read poem after poem, trying to soak up what was in them that created the impact. The harder I worked at studying them, the more frustrated I became. There must be a trick to it. All I had to do was break the code.

I think the answer came out of fatigue rather than diligence, from giving up the desire to analyze. When I lost interest in picking apart the lines and just let the feeling work its way inside, it was right there. It was in every poem but hidden in the background. What was left out was as important as what was put in.

I approached the poems differently from then on. Before writing, I observed. As I observed, I felt. From feeling came connection, out of connection, a poem.

The bridge Haiku built between me and poetry led me into the joy of other forms and the challenge of free verse where the form is designed by the intention. Poetry stopped being irrelevant. More than that, I started paying attention to the hidden in everyday life that brought out normally unconscious associations. Haiku opened me to exploring new pathways within myself leading, perhaps, to higher connections.

> On the pristine lawn
> a dandelion grows
> all by itself.

> Dolores Kozielski

Bela the Bat

My husband found a bat on our back doorstep. It was a wide-winged, brown-haired, full-bodied bat. It hung onto the doorframe with its bat fingers and whenever we went too near, it made a bat hiss that sounded like a cross between a cicada and a snake. Its face was human-like, with eyes that followed our every movement.

It was easy to understand why the bat was associated with evil. There was Count Dracula daring us to come closer. We did. Step. Hissss. We backed away. Even though we were many times its size, that bat intimidated us.

We started calling the bat Bela Lugosi. It would not have surprised us if it suddenly turned into the vampire of our childhood horror films. I was glad our children were away – grownups with creeps were difficult, but spooked kids would be impossible.

We phoned the local nature center for advice on how to proceed. The naturalist said that bats don't usually fly out in bright sunlight or come too near people so the bat was probably sick. It might fly away or it might die.

Could someone take it away?

Not on Sunday. We should call back tomorrow.

Was there something we could do in the meantime?

It was best not to touch it; it could have rabies.

We firmly bolted the door and tried to ignore our unbidden guest, but every couple of minutes one of us invented a reason to go around back to peek at it. We returned with reports.

"Bela isn't acting right," I said.

"What's right for a bat?" said Michael.

"How should I know? He just doesn't look right."

"His wings are droopy."

"He isn't hanging on any more. He's just lying there."

"I think he's dying.

"Should I poke him to see if he moves?"

"Leave him alone. Any creature has the right to die with dignity."

Before going to sleep, we peered down at him from our bedroom window, focusing a flashlight's beam on the limp body.

"Should we leave a light on for him?" I asked. "The kids always like to have a light on when they're sick."

"Don't be silly. Bats like the dark."

We checked on Bela first thing in the morning, hoping he had flown off into his natural nighttime environment. He was there, a hairy, still offering at our door.

"He's gone," Michael said.

"I know."

For some reason, there was a catch in my voice. I scooped up Bela with a garden trowel while Michael dug a hole in our backyard cemetery where the deceased fish, gerbils, hamsters, and parakeets of a lifetime of pet-keeping rested. Now I wished the kids were home; from practice, they knew how to put on a good funeral.

"Go in peace, Bela," I said to our bat.

I picked up a handful of dirt and scattered it over his body. We finished burying him and walked toward the house. The back entrance was usable again, bat free and back to normal.

Only not quite.

I reached for the comfort of Michael's hand.

"Something doesn't feel right," I said.

"What's right for a doorstep?" Michael asked.

"I don't know. Something is missing. There's an emptiness."

We looked briefly at where Bela had lain, then stepped respectfully over the threshold.

Show and Tell

As workshop leader for a teen arts program, I was required to read stories submitted in advance by middle school students, offer suggestions, and share some of the craft of writing in a workshop setting. I began reading the day I received their stories and almost immediately wondered if I was going to be able to do the job. It wasn't the quality of the work that concerned me; some of the writers were truly talented while others were writing at an age appropriate level. It was the intimacy of it.

There were the expected fanciful stories about space aliens and magical boxes but there were also stories of personal tragedy. One young girl wrote of how she never told her grandfather she loved him before he died. Another described painful feelings of inadequacy. There was violence in their stories and love. While I could not determine how much was shear creation, I knew that the same emotions were needed to write truth or fiction. What right had I to listen in on their young lives?

I wrote notes on each story, giving positive suggestions and encouragement. It wasn't in my job description but I wanted to ease some of the pain that came through the pages.

On the eve of the workshop, I sought last minute inspiration for something to offer this group of teenagers who had become intimate strangers in my life. I sat quietly and listened to the stillness. From it came the understanding that while most of my audience would benefit from the workshop, there was one particular person who needed to hear what I would say. I had no idea what that might be.

In the morning, I dutifully packed up their stories and headed off to meet my teens. Thirty students and two of their teachers crowded into a small classroom in the local college where the program was being held. As I handed back their manuscripts, I tried to connect the words with the faces but found they didn't match. The grief-stricken writer had an angel's face, fair and serene with untroubled eyes. The author of a beautiful descriptive essay had a haunted look. I wondered which one I was supposed to reach.

Then things got busy; there was no time for wondering. We started exploring our surroundings and playing with words. We talked about how to make descriptions more vivid.

"Remember Show and Tell when you were in elementary school?" I asked.

"Hey, yeah," said a boy. "That was fun. I got to show the Lego space station I made."

The writer of the alien story.

"I once brought in my pet snake," said a girl, "and let everyone touch it."

"The reason we all loved Show and Tell was that we could see things right there. We could touch and smell them, really know them. That's what a writer must help the reader to do. But there is only the page on which to do it. Everything must be sensed through the words."

I used a boy and the girl sitting behind him to illustrate how to show emotions rather than tell about them.

"We could say that "Rob" likes "Sarah." End of story. Or we could say that when Rob sees Sarah at the hall locker, he turns the color of a cherry lollipop."

The boy and the girl both blushed as the class whistled.

Then everyone settled down to adding descriptive details to the scene.

We were playing the writer's version of Show and Tell.

When the session ended, I smiled them out the door. They seemed to have a good time. Maybe they even learned something. I hoped I did enough and prayed I did no harm.

As I was preparing to leave, one of the teachers came back.

"What made you choose that particular boy, the one you called Rob, to illustrate your point?" she asked.

"I don't know," I said. "It just felt right."

To be honest, until that moment, I hadn't known I was going to use that example. So much of a workshop presentation is spontaneous depending upon the members and dynamics of the group.

"Well, I want you to know that you made a huge difference in his life. He is from a special education class and the thing he most needed was to be accorded the same attention and respect that all the other students take for granted. You did that for him."

"It wasn't intentional," I said, knowing I couldn't take credit for it.

"It doesn't matter. If you do nothing else today, I want you to know that this is what you were here for. Thank you."

I packed the rest of my belongings and left the room as the next group was entering.

There was one person who needed to hear what I had to say. I was grateful that I was guided to say it.

LANGUAGES

LANGUAGES

I grew up, linguistically, in three parts of the world. The European side of my family spoke Yiddish, the Middle-Eastern side spoke Arabic and the people in my American community spoke English. Each language group was distinct from the others. It not only encompassed sound but body language, relationships, emotions, customs and history. When I was with one group, I responded differently than I did when I was with the others.

I was sensitive to the nuances that were unique to each. I learned quickly that with Grandma Rose, my Yiddish-speaking grandmother, I talked first and ate later. Food was a tool used to reward, compensate, punish, or console. With Sitaw, my Arabic-speaking grandmother, I ate first and spoke later. Food was given immediately as a sign of hospitality. In my English-speaking friends' houses, we ate and spoke at the same time, food being part of the social process.

I didn't realize until recently how I tuned my listening to the unspoken parts of language. During a vacation in Paris, my friend Claire, who had practiced her high school French and was able to put sentences together to ask questions, took on the function of talking to the clerks, concierges, waiters, and other Parisians with whom we interacted. When they answered, however, she was overwhelmed by the rapid speech and could not translate. While I did not feel comfortable speaking my substandard French, I always knew what was being said. Some of that understanding came through gesture and exaggeration, some through occasionally recognized words, but the major part was received through intention – the speaker's intention to communicate and mine to comprehend. Claire and I laughed about how together we made up one tourist.

It is this intention, I believe, that is the important component of language. It removes the biggest barrier to communication – the ego. I notice that if I am focused on my end of an interchange, whether it is spoken or otherwise, I miss most of what is actually being said. Certainly I miss the nuances, the clues, that tell more of the story than the words. Taking a breath, a simple five-second pause, before participating in an exchange helps to relax the ego and puts me in a more receptive space. So does focusing less on how I can understand and more on what needs to be understood. This helps the ego pay attention to something other than itself.

Intention allows us to connect not only with other people but also with other aspects of ourselves, to use our intuition. Intuition, in turn, and telepathy can only be heard when the inner controller is napping or momentarily occupied.

My desire to share in the many language forms comes not so much from wanting to be a citizen of the world, although my childhood started me along that road, than to be one of the universe. As technology shrinks our world and expands our perception, the intention to communicate becomes the most important language of all. Then, as we go beyond national speech into the heart of universal connection, the many languages that have separated us become transformed into one language that unites us all.

The Sixth Language

My grandfather spoke five languages in varying degrees of proficiency: Arabic, which was his first language, Hebrew, Spanish, French, and English least of all. I loved him because of his great kindness although I had trouble talking with him. I sat at his table and mostly listened, trying to pick up the meaning of conversations from the guttural Arabic syllables.

I learned the names of food from my grandmother because the females in the family spent most of the time in the kitchen preparing the holiday feasts, but that was the extent of my bilingual education. My father was too busy to teach me the language and my mother didn't know it.

I asked my father once to tell me how to say I love you in Arabic. I said it to my grandfather the next week. His eyes widened and he laughed such a hearty laugh that I thought his thin body might shake itself apart. I didn't know if I had said it incorrectly or if he was just surprised I had spoken in Arabic at all. I felt my face redden. He must have seen my discomfort because he patted my shoulder and nodded his head vigorously. I wished I knew the right words.

When his first great-grandchild, my sister's son, was born, my grandfather was delighted. He sat David on his lap and bounced him up and down as he hummed strange, beguiling tunes. David looked deeply into his eyes as they sat contentedly together for long periods of time.

One day, David saw an old drum high on top of the china cabinet. He pointed to it. My grandfather reached up and lovingly handed it to his great-grandson. David banged happily on the taut skin before he gave it back.

My grandfather tapped it with his bony fingers. David clapped. More tapping, more clapping. Then David started to dance. My grandfather drummed rhythms to the movement then joined in. From then on, each time David visited there was drumming and dancing. Everyone would laugh. *Isn't that cute?* they said. But something more than cute was going on.

David, like his mother and aunt, never learned Arabic. He was three years old when his great-grandfather, the grandfather I loved across a chasm of unspoken language, died. He shouldn't have remembered the drumming and dancing but he did and does still.

I think it is possible that my grandfather spoke six languages. He was most fluent in the one that required no words.

Bird Talk

I sat, restless, in the bright shade of a fading afternoon on my backyard bench. The sun was relentless that summer, not even letting a cloud hint of possible rain. The swamp maple, usually an effective parasol, could only offer intermittent reprieve with its wilted leaves. I was bored and wanted to do something – visit a friend, go on a picnic, take a walk, anything – but it was too hot.

The heat pressed against my skin and I wondered if I should make my way back to the cool house but late day inertia had set in. Except for the bounce, bounce of a sweat-soaked leg, I didn't move.

I heard a bird twit somewhere in the tree but I was too heat-burdened to look for the source. Then it twitted again, more insistently. I looked up. It was a robin, not far off, about six feet away in the crotch of a low hanging branch. Twit. Twit.

The bird was looking down at me. I imitated its call. It called back. I could hardly keep up my responses before it would initiate another set of twitters. It hopped to another branch, still chatting and carefully watching me. I answered. It stayed within my sight. There were other birds in the yard but this one mesmerized me. We were having a conversation. *Good boy*, I thought, at least I can talk to you.

The robin flew to the ground and walked back and forth as it continued to chatter. By this time, the heat was beyond oppressive. It was too hot to move even my leg, and too much effort to twit, so I watched the robin silently. It came closer, never losing eye contact. I had the strange feeling it was sizing me up.

When it flew to the privet hedge off to the right, I lost sight of it. An instant later, I heard it call again. Softer, more gently, an answering call came from within the bushes. I spotted the robin again, moving through the leaves until it came to a clump in the twigs. A nest! And there was the object of its call, an almost grown bird-child.

I was startled. In the few minutes I had been aware of the bird, I had made a number of assumptions: that it was male, that we were twitting about pleasantries, that we were experiencing a friendly encounter between species. I gasped at the magnitude of my arrogance. I had heard but I had not listened. The bird was female. She was not trying to engage me in idle conversation but quite deliberately attempting to warn me away from her child. Only after assessing that I was harmless (and probably a bit slow-witted) did she continue about the business of being a mother bird.

I learned something valuable on that bench, in the simmering heat that insisted I sit still. It was a lesson that bypassed my thoughts, ran deeper than my comprehension, was aside from my intelligence, a lesson that could only be absorbed by sitting quietly and listening to a bird.

Universal Party Line

Dolores and I were curious. Could we communicate telepathically? We decided to experiment. Every day at 8:30 in the morning, we sat quietly in our houses three doors away and for fifteen minutes sent each other images. For the first five minutes, she broadcast while I received. The next five minutes, I sent and she listened. The last five minutes we both tuned in to see if we would pick up anything when we weren't transmitting.

A clock. A yellow rose. A hand. A word. We got them all. It must be too easy, we thought. Let's do something harder.

We sent scenes – a dog running in the park, a girl gathering wildflowers. I saw the dog's red tongue and Dolores saw buttercups. I would try to trick her by imagining something ordinary but slightly out of kilter. I sent her an American flag with the stripes running vertically.

"I got the strangest picture," she said. It was exactly what I had sent.

Still too easy. We would not divide the time, we decided. We would just sit and see what happens.

When we compared notes, it was as if we were each dreaming and the dreams we told each other were the same! We got messages and both knew the words. She would start describing her visions and I would fill in the details. We felt each other's feelings, heard each other's songs.

One day I forgot our appointment. At 8:30, I was in the shower under a stream of cleansing hot water. When I realized what time it was, the fifteen minutes was almost up. I just thought of Dolores without words, without pictures.

Later that day she told me that she hadn't picked up anything for most of the time we were supposed to be sitting but then she suddenly felt as if she was standing under a waterfall. She described the water cascading over her head and trickling down her body. She described my shower.

We stopped our experiment. We had proven to ourselves that telepathic communication was possible. We also realized that we were on a universal party line with no controls except our own. It suddenly became important to be careful what we broadcast and to monitor what we might pick up.

The Universe knows no privacy and takes no responsibility.

Sharing Combs

Sandy and I are fairly recent friends by earth time. We met nine years ago when we enrolled in a holistic studies program at a local college. The first night was unexpectedly rainy. I was parked across campus and by the time I entered the building, I was dripping, my hair plastered to my head. Sandy, who had arrived earlier and had the foresight to carry an umbrella, reached into her purse and took out a comb.

"I never lend anyone my comb," she said as she handed it to me.

I looked into her steady eyes.

"I never borrow anyone's comb," I said as I ran it through my drenched hair.

It had the feeling of a ritual, the offering and accepting, an acknowledgment of a relationship recognized on an unconscious level.

Still, it took a while for the conscious awareness to catch up. We were given repeated demonstrations of our connection. Once, when we were learning Foot Reflexology, we found ourselves paired as partners for practice. It was getting late so we decided to save time and work on each other simultaneously.

I sat with my right leg on her left knee while her right leg rested on my left knee. We massaged each other's feet and discovered that the same spots on our feet were sore. When we finished the massage, we noticed that both our left feet were their normal color but our right feet were bright red.

We asked our instructor about it. He was amazed. He had never seen that before. He said that we had created a loop of our energy and reacted as if we were one person. We laughed about it. It made a good story.

Soon we began to pick up on little things that, by themselves, would seem like coincidences but together formed a pattern. Sandy would feel confused one day and a week later I wouldn't even know my own name. She would tell me that she was getting swamped with phone calls from people asking for advice. Within the month I would wonder if *my* phone number had been emblazoned on some giant billboard. I would suddenly feel compelled to start an exercise program and wouldn't be able to reach Sandy because she was out walking. When I recommended a book I thought she should read, Sandy told me that a friend had just sent it to her in the mail.

We started getting messages for each other in meditation. Sandy called to tell me the reason I was feeling uncomfortable was that I had released old thoughts and had not yet accepted the new ones that replaced them. I hadn't told her about the fog that was shrouding my brain. I sensed I was in a new space with no reference points. I was drifting, anchorless. It was a very uncomfortable place to be. She lifted me.

I told Sandy that she was a star illuminating everything she encountered. People were drawn to her, felt brighter in her presence. She was not to doubt the healing effect she brought to others. She was glad for the message because just that morning she wondered if she was doing what she was meant to do. I grounded her.

We reminded each other that we had no idea of what we were saying. We knew that the messages were not coming from us personally but from a broader perspective. We understood and valued the words that came through.

It is inconceivable to us now that there was a time when we weren't aware of each other. If Sandy and I are connected in this way, might there be others, not yet recognized, waiting to become reacquainted? Are we not all acquainted on some level?

How many combs are offered and because of convention, because we all too often listen only to the words being said, are not accepted?

Horse, Horse, Tiger, Tiger

One summer, my family went to China. No one spoke Mandarin, the official Chinese language. At our request, our Shanghai guide taught us how to say *Hello, Goodbye,* and *Thank you.* The Chinese people like to bargain, she said, so she also taught us to say, *How much is that?* and *That's too expensive.* We learned the Chinese equivalent of *so-so,* which would make it seem as if we were not too eager to buy and we would not be cheated. What she didn't teach us, and perhaps couldn't, was how to listen with Chinese ears.

In America, we accept many different pronunciations and still understand what is meant; it is the word itself that conveys its meaning. In China, it is the tone of the character that makes the word and, depending upon which is used, the meaning changes. The character *ma*, for instance, can mean you are calling your mother, asking a question, naming a horse, or saying something offensive.

So, armed with our new linguistic knowledge, we headed off on our own into the shops that lined Nanjing Road, a major shopping area in Shanghai. In one shop, we pointed to a fan. The clerk took it from its case to show to us. We looked it over and carefully said in our best Mandarin, "Mao, mao, hoo, hoo." The clerk's eyes widened. She backed away into the protection of the other clerks who were standing around stone-faced trying to decipher our intentions. Afraid that we were creating an international incident, we quickly bought the fan and forgot the bargaining. We tried our language skills in another store. This time the clerk burst into laughter and repeated our statement loud enough for everyone around the dimly lit counter to hear. They all laughed. We still didn't get it.

We were laughed out of a few more stores in a few more cities before we stopped trying to bargain. We couldn't figure out what was wrong. We said what our guide had taught us, hadn't we?

We finally asked another guide in the resort city of Hanghzou why we were getting such reactions. When he heard what we said, he laughed, too.

"What you are saying is, 'Horse, horse, tiger, tiger'."

He pronounced the words slowly for us to hear the right way to say them. We listened very carefully this time and said the phrase exactly as he taught us.

"No, no. That is not right."

We tried again with equally disastrous results. We couldn't hear the difference. A dip in intonation, if we heard it at all was, for us, just another way of speaking – for our guide it was a whole new word. He shook his head and gave up.

We stopped verbally bargaining for the rest of the trip but found that through gesture and intensity, we were able to purchase what we wanted without feeling we were being taken advantage of too badly. And we were rewarded with smiles instead of laughs.

Somewhere along the way, we were told that the few words we knew were spoken with a Shanghai accent. We didn't try to figure out the regional variations; we were still stuck on horses and tigers.

Inner City Stories

I spent an intense four days in an inner city elementary school talking to children about writing. We discussed how to get an idea for a story, how a story is developed, how it is prepared for a book. We created special characters and then gave them lives. We listed what they liked to eat, what they liked to do. We put down how many brothers and sisters they had and where they lived. We gave them personalities. Then we put them into stories.

Some stories the children wrote on their own, others we wrote together. Sometimes the stories were fantasy as when "Golddust the Snake" hid under the covers and everyone in the kindergarten class went looking for him.

Sometimes the stories came from the everyday lives of the writers. One class gave "Crazy Toes Turtle" a beeper. Another said the character had a Spanish-speaking sister. There was a story about Crazy Toes meeting a strange girl who tried to convince him they were brother and sister although they had never met. The students could relate to his confusion because so many of them had that same experience.

One third-grade girl wrote a story but it wasn't about the character the class created. She waved her hand frantically, desperate to read. Her story told of six women who had no place to live, no place to go. They knocked on someone's door and asked the man who answered if they could come in and live with him. He said yes, they could come in because he could tell they were good people.

Another class wrote a long story about "Brandy the Mouse Queen" who became a very rich rock star. Her husband had left her years ago so she married another man who swindled her out of all her money and then ran away.

"Lisa the Rabbit" was nice but sometimes she did mean things.

"Baby Jack" had a brother and sister who teased him until he cried.

I heard stories about sad and broken families and about violence. There were stories that had a beginning and a middle but seemed to have no end.

As the stories emerged, I listened with a sympathetic ear but it was clear to me that I needed to listen underneath the words that were often read haltingly, with great seriousness as befitted the subjects. I heard something else, too. I heard the humor that came with the worry and the delight at finding a new family member. These young people had compassion for those in need and rejoiced in hope renewed at finding a resolution to the story's problem.

Everyone wanted to read. Those who wrote together read together, gaining strength in the sound of the partner speaking. The shy ones read with their heads down in soft voices. The bold ones read loudly, enjoying the attention.

I was standing next to a girl who had just told us that the story really happened and went on to read about her character who went to the hospital because she had a broken arm. I missed part of her story because I was suddenly struck with the beauty of her spirit. Her eyes were brilliant with the excitement of reading her own words. Her face was shining in her unselfconscious preoccupation.

I saw her light and knew that regardless of her circumstances or her skill, besides her gawkiness or the whispering behind hands from the rest of the class, she was a child of the Universe. Each of us in the room, in the school, on the planet, was a being of light seeking a way to shine. I was aware that to truly hear, it was not enough to let our ears listen to the words; it was more important for the heart to listen to the reaching of the soul.

DREAMS

DREAMS

I saw a painting in an art show that took my breath away. It is "The Leap" by Boston artist Damon Lehrer. The scene is of five teenagers in the foreground of a city. Two girls are on the right, looking down. A boy and a girl are on the left, pressed together but not embracing. There are no smiles on their faces and their eyes seem deadened by their surroundings. A harsh tableau. In the center, a boy wearing rollerblades is caught mid-leap between the pairs. His arms are outstretched and he is facing in the opposite direction from the others, away from their resignation and despair. In that leap is life and hope. In that leap is a dream.

We all have dreams when we are young. It seems as if life is made of dreams – choosing the ideal career, meeting the right partner, making a difference in the world, living a worthy existence. Some of us give up on our dreams along the way while others fulfill them. Then there are those, regardless of age, who continue to generate dreams that make their lives fuller and richer, that expand them into bigger spaces.

When I looked at that painting, I wondered what the boy was hearing that was different from his companions. What was the artist feeling when he picked up his brush to give shape to a dream? Did he listen to critics and begin to doubt himself? Was this the way he conceived the painting or did he change it while the idea and paint were still wet with possibility?

Dreams need to be flexible to stay alive. They are changing creations that grow with the dreamer. Childhood dreams that don't mature become confining cages instead of inspirations.

It isn't easy to leap into a dream or from one dream to another. The boy in the painting is vulnerable – his arms are open to the unknown and he has no footing. My heart goes out to him, not in fear that he will fall but in faith that he won't. My inner voice tells me he will succeed because he sees beyond the concrete and the sadness, higher than the buildings that form the city skyline. He is suspended, captured for that second, in the expanse of the Universe.

I want to leap, too! Maybe if I am open to listening to the inner voice that says I can do it, I will have the courage to push off from my boundaries. Perhaps if I am persistent, I will lift my dreams into reality. Then it might just be possible to transform, as Damon Lehrer has with his leaper, living into a work of art.

Serious Work

My husband says I don't work very hard. It hurts me when he says that. I wonder if he respects what I do. I write. He likes the idea of my writing but my methods seem to baffle him.

When I am upstairs, he peeks through my partially closed office door and sees me playing solitaire or reading or sitting in meditation. I put my foot up as I type. Maybe I push back in my chair and stare out the window at the brown oak leaves still clinging to winter branches.

His office doesn't have a window. He says it is too distracting.

Sometimes I go out and work with my friend down the street. We write in her basement, sitting on bar stools. We laugh a lot when we write. I make the mistake of telling him how much fun we have.

That is not the way to get things done, he says. To him, I am not serious about my work.

If he catches me when I am having trouble with one of my stories, I think maybe he is right, maybe I am fooling myself about being a writer. I consider going out and getting a real job, in an office, with regular hours and weekly pay.

I drink a cup of Dragon Well tea as I ponder this idea of doing serious work. My eyes are drawn to the fourteen published books propped up on the mantle. I remember the five more that have been sold and will one day find their way to my doorstep, to booksellers' shelves, to libraries, and to the hands of my readers. Then I go back upstairs to face the seven books that are in various stages of completion in the memory of my computer.

As I watch the leaves flutter in the sharp afternoon breeze, I suddenly know how to fix the story. I type furiously until I hear my husband's voice call up, "What's for dinner?"

"Whatever you want to make," I yell down.

I can't take the time to play with pasta, not now. The words are flowing, the characters are interacting, the plot is building to a crescendo.

His workday is finished but mine has only begun. I have just created a whole world. How much more serious can work get?

Church Traveling

Felicia church-travels. She goes from one church to another listening and hoping for the words that tell her this is a place where truth is spoken, where there are no boundaries, where all people are God's.

When the minister says that those who do not believe in what he preaches are going to Hell, she stands and says, "What was that you said? Did I hear you right? Did I hear you say that some of God's children are going to Hell?"

The next week she is in another church.

Sometimes she vows not to open her mouth no matter what the minister says. She can't stay quiet, though. When the light that shines through the windows doesn't enter the minister's heart, she must speak. Her eyes blazing with her own inner light, she challenges, questions. "You can't mean what you just said!"

The next week, a new church, and another hope.

Changed Dreams

When she was three years old, my daughter told me she wanted ballet lessons. I didn't know where Stephanie got that idea. We had never borrowed ballet books from the library. She wasn't in school yet and we had just moved to a new neighborhood so she wasn't playing with anyone who went to ballet school.

She certainly didn't get any feeling for ballet from me. I didn't know anything about it. I had been to only one ballet performance in my life and that experience was an unappreciated gift to see Swan Lake with Natalia Makarova and Rudolph Nureyev. I was so ignorant of the art, I nearly fell asleep watching two of the world's greatest dancers.

I let the request pass the way grownups ignore so much of children's talk.

Stephanie persisted. I watched her dance on the balcony of our apartment. She twirled in what I later learned were pirouettes. She stretched her body long as she balanced on one leg – an elementary arabesque. I wondered where she learned the steps, how she knew such expressive ways to move her body.

Finally, after a year of asking, I took her to a ballet school. She learned rapidly. It was as if she was remembering rather than learning.

She outgrew the school quickly. I became a chauffeur to other schools as she progressed. She was dancing five times a week and spent her summers at the ballet studio. I offered her camp but she wasn't interested. Ballet got her through the bullies at junior high and the boredom of high school. She had a passion for dancing that stunned me.

Then one day she stopped. She packed up her pointe shoes, put away her leg warmers, and stepped off the stage.

By now, ballet had become part of my life. My daughter had educated me about ballet through her participation. I understood what I was seeing. I knew the steps. I followed news of the companies. What I wouldn't have given to see that performance of Swan Lake now!

I found myself grieving and wrote poems about the years I spent attending performances and helping backstage. What was I to do with the space that had been opened inside me that could now only be filled with dance? I found the photograph of her baby arabesques and hid it away to sneak confused glances at when nostalgia swept over me.

Stephanie went off to college but did not choose a performing arts school. She fiddled around a little with modern dance but didn't want me to see the performances. Soon she stopped dancing completely. The only ballets she spoke of were those she saw from the velvet seats in the audience.

"Why?" I once asked when she was visiting.

Stephanie looked at me tenderly as I were the child, "Don't you tell me to listen inside?" she said.

I nodded.

"Well, I listened. I stopped because it wasn't enough for me any more. The inner fire to do it had cooled. I needed something else."

Stephanie found that she liked working with children. She wanted to share things with them and help them to explore things for themselves. As an assistant teacher at a pre-school one year, she worried about how to get through to a girl who had no social skills beyond hitting and grabbing what she wanted and to the boy who was so smart he needed a daily challenge like a multi-vitamin pill. She went back to school and now embraced teaching as enthusiastically as she had ballet.

She hugged me.

"I have to listen to what I'm feeling, don't I? If you don't listen, how do you know what to do? How do you know who you are?"

When my daughter left, I took out the photo and looked at it one last time. Then I put it away with the remainder of my sadness over what I thought was the lost dream of a three-year-old I never understood. The dream was not lost but changed. She was still educating me.

Blake's Vision

Blake, at sixteen, had the soul of a poet. He wrote songs about the difficult passage from youth into adulthood. The songs told of losing life's vision to worldly responsibility. They questioned what was cool and what wasn't and mocked the rituals teens went through to be accepted. You're not crazy, they cried out, to want to keep innocence alive.

While his friends strummed their guitars to hard rock tunes of love and hate, Blake picked intricate melodies that gave physical substance to his metaphysical themes. He composed ten songs in a week then worried that he would forget the music because he didn't write it down. He taped one song painstakingly on cassette until he was happy with the results knowing that he would probably change it next week anyway, if he found a chord he liked better.

"Hey," his friends would say. "What's up this weekend?"

"I'm writing and recording," he would answer.

"Sure, that's all you ever do," they'd grumble.

For Blake, with school and his job, there seemed little enough time for his music. He composed when the music was flowing and worried when it wasn't. He didn't want to be a one-song writer, a one-album recorder. Every day he wrote down titles, subjects, snippets of ideas that miraculously formed themselves into songs. He wasn't sure where it all came from but who cared? Just let it be there.

He used to belong to a band but quit. They said he was too bossy, always wanting things his way. Blake saw it differently; they were playing his songs – he just wanted them to express his vision.

That Blake had a vision was clear. It was visible in the spark of his eyes. It was apparent from the intensity of the notes pulsing through his bedroom door. A listener could get lost in the ripples of blue-green sound in his song "Sink" and forget that, at sixteen, Blake was only beginning to dream.

SINK

Sink
To the bottom of the ocean floor

Think
If you would like to stay

For the mermaid parade
Watch them float and wave their fins

I think
You'll be happy in this land

Blink your eyes
To make sure

All you see is real
And you're not insane
Under the moonlight comes the rain.

Words and music by Blake Marshall-Attle

WAVELENGTHS

WAVELENGTHS

On the way from Philadelphia to New York, somewhere around Exit 8 on the New Jersey Turnpike, the radio stations begin to switch. Music takes on the staccato rhythm of static. Talk shows start to resemble Mad Libs as words from new programs insinuate themselves into the fading ones. The deep male voice of a campaigning politician can turn into the soprano of a female scatting jazz while an advertisement for oriental carpets might just end up selling perfume. Whether it is caused by one radio frequency leaving and another trying to take its place or by two stations on the same frequency but in different areas, the result is the same – confused communication.

Most of the time I am amused by the random juxtapositions but sometimes I get annoyed when a program becomes garbled and no amount of tuning brings it back. It reminds me of some of the discussions I've had where I think the person I'm talking with is in the same thought-space I am but then she says something and I realize she is broadcasting on another station. We'll talk in and out of each other's words until either we lock in on one frequency or one station fades out completely. It may happen that we don't connect at all and then the attempt at communicating will have failed.

I find this occurs particularly with family members. We spend so much time in the seemingly same environment that surely we must know it in the same way. That's not necessarily true. The stations my sister and I listen to are, and have always been, different. They are encoded by our personalities and perceptions, our needs and desires. We enhance each other's memory of events through our individual points of view.

As difficult as it is to tune in to a close family member, it can be that much harder to understand a friend, a neighbor, an acquaintance, a business associate, a stranger. The common ground is more distant, making it first necessary to find the radio before being able to deal with the factors of station, time and program. Scientists have been trying to communicate with aliens for decades while we are alien to each other right here on Earth.

But we, ourselves, are the most challenging stations of all to tune in. I wonder what I really know about myself. I get static from a constant barrage of thoughts and my mind flips frequencies at whim, especially if I am faced with something I'd rather not examine at the moment.

If we have so much trouble communicating with each other and with ourselves, how is it even possible to contact the frequency that we think of as our higher self or soul?

Actually, it is easier than we think. When two frequencies are close together, as we are with our higher selves, then the stronger of the two prevails. Instead of dialing around like crazy looking for the right program, all we need do is allow the signal to bring us to it.

To do that, we need to provide a clear receiver. I try to stay receptive to messages from my higher self by lessening the interference. I practice quiet sitting and calm myself by watching the flow of my breath. I take walks outside and attune myself to the rhythm of my steps. I focus on one thing at a time and when other things interrupt, I gently but firmly tune them out. I eat foods that balance me while I stay away from those that clog my system and fog my brain.

I make the effort to keep the airwaves open because I want as much information as I can acquire so I can make the best decisions on how to live my life. The physical radio I am listening through may age and look worn but I am constantly refining the inner workings. Each time I listen to my higher self, I raise my frequency and elevate myself.

If we all tune into the universal frequency, we might learn to appreciate the different frequencies humanity represents. We might broaden our understanding of nature, human and otherwise, and function in a more compassionate way toward all life. We would be meeting all aspects of existence on the same wavelength and that is where we experience true communication.

Sisters

I love my sister. I know she loves me. That's the closest we get to similarity. People who meet us are amazed that we're sisters. We look nothing like each other. We think differently. Our viewpoints are often at odds. Although we do things together, we respond in different ways.

We were having tea together the other day when we started talking about our childhood.

"Do you remember how Mom used to wear jeans before they were fashionable?" Ronnie asked.

"The only time I remember her wearing jeans was when she was shoveling snow," I said.

"Oh, no. She wore them all the time. I thought I'd die if one of my friends saw her."

"I never cared what she wore," I said. "What drove *me* nuts was Dad's wake-up music."

"His what?"

"Wake-up music. Don't you remember, every Saturday he blasted music from the big console radio downstairs to wake us up?"

"Why would he do that?"

"Because he was up and wanted company. How could you forget something like that?"

My sister shrugged. "One thing I'll never forget," she said, "is the time Dad took a photo of Mom with a blob of makeup on her nose. Boy, was that funny."

"It wasn't Dad who took the picture, it was our neighbor. I was embarrassed for Mom."

"Well, I guess you had to be there," Ronnie said.

The point is, I *was* there. And she was in the house when our father sent polkas pulsing loudly upstairs at eight o'clock in the morning. Why were our memories so different?

"You were always the sensitive one," Ronnie said as she refilled our tea mugs. I was drinking green tea; she had hazelnut vanilla. "You never hurt anyone's feelings."

"What about the time I imitated Jackie Gleason and called Grandma a mental case?" I said.

"You didn't!"

"You were popular," I countered. "I was jealous of you for a while."

"Of what? My frizzy hair? I wanted straight hair like yours."

"You had dates. Someone proposed to you when you were fourteen! No one even asked me out until ninth grade."

"Go on."

"It's true. You wanted a Sweet Sixteen party in a fancy restaurant. I wanted no party at all."

"I loved parties."

"I hated them."

"Did you feel poor?" Ronnie asked. "I thought we had serious money troubles because Dad was working three jobs and Mom worked, too."

"I never thought about it. I knew they worked hard but I didn't feel deprived."

"Is it possible," she said, "that we actually lived through the same childhood? In the same family? In the same house? We sound like strangers."

My sister sipped at her half-empty mug of tea.

"What's your favorite memory?" she asked.

I thought for a moment, the half-full mug mid-way to my lips.

"The car rides," I said emphatically. "Remember when we drove through the countryside and Dad..."

"Made the car dance," she said. "We all sang, 'Down by the old, mill stream...'"

"And 'You are my sunshine, my only sunshine...'"

"You make me haappyyy," she chimed in, "when skies are graaay."

"Our harmony was terrible."

We laughed at our voices, which hadn't improved at all over the years. We could feel the car jerking in rhythm as our father alternately pressed and released the gas pedal.

"Yes, I remember," my sister said.

We luxuriated in the rare common memory.

Then we hugged hurriedly as she dashed upstairs to dress for a dinner date and I rushed off to my Yoga class.

Aliens

Sometimes I imagine that everyone on earth is really an alien from outer space. No two aliens come from the same place. Each place has an atmosphere, physical environment, animals, insects, and plants different from those I know. Each alien comes from a society that is unfamiliar to me in its organizations, family groupings, relationships, and customs. Each alien's molecular structure and nerve circuitry is unknown. Because of all the differences, I cannot truly know what an alien wants, how it thinks, what it thinks, what it needs, how it feels, why it is here. The only thing I know is that it looks human and it has this tremendous desire to communicate with me.

It tries to use my language but sometimes it lapses into its native tongue and I can't understand it at all. The alien's ideas sound like gibberish to me. I find that I am often frustrated because I can't tell it exactly what I mean so misunderstandings and arguments occur.

The alien, too, gets frustrated when it feels I'm not listening and that only makes it harder to forge a connection.

Understanding an alien takes work. I listen closely not only to what the alien is saying but also to how it is saying it. I am patient without rushing in with my own interpretation of what it is trying to tell me. I am attentive to its body language even though its body is not exactly like mine. I can sense what it is feeling, if I allow myself to be open to the inner alien.

I look deeply into its eyes and realize that there is so much to share that cannot be said in words.

I try not to be startled when I finally understand that it cannot know what I want, how I think, what I need, how I feel, or why I am here because to *it* I am the alien.

Eavesdropping

I was taught not to eavesdrop. It isn't polite. Yet I found myself eavesdropping on myself one day, listening in to what I was saying, watching my actions as if I were another person.

There was a noise in the house last week. I was upstairs. By myself. Not five minutes before, I had let in a postal worker. It was too cold for him to be waiting outside as I made out a check for the C.O.D. parcel. We talked as I signed my name in two places. When he left, I closed and locked the door, I thought, and went back to my office on the second floor.

The noise sounded like a door opening.

I am never afraid in my house. Still, I went downstairs again to reassure myself that the door was locked. It wasn't. Had I forgotten? Surely not. A strange sense of panic welled up and a stranger sense of separation. I was experiencing the panic on an emotional level but not physically or mentally. I calmly went to the kitchen and took a knife from the drawer.

What are you doing? I asked myself.

I will protect myself, I answered silently.

Interesting.

I went from room to room, opening closets, looking behind chairs. All the while I held the knife, I watched myself holding it. This was quite surprising for an avowed pacifist.

Will you use it? Can you use it? I wondered.

I don't know.

I peeked into the furnace room and the walk-in storage closet in the basement.

Why are you doing this?
Curious, isn't it?

The inner dialogue continued as I checked behind the shower curtain. Back of the sofa. Under the bed. In all the bedrooms.

You can put the knife away any time you choose, I heard myself say.

I continued my search as I watched myself searching.

The garage was filled with boxes and lawn machines but empty of an intruder. The laundry room provided no hiding spaces. There was nowhere else to look. I walked up the stairs to my office, locked the door for the first time, and put the knife within easy reach on my desk.

Then, as suddenly as the panic arose, it was over.

What was that all about? I said aloud.

I returned the knife to its usual place among the assorted mixing spoons, spatulas, skewers, and cookie cutters. The question lingered – What *was* that all about? Was I capable of harming another human being even under extreme circumstances? I hadn't thought so until now. Was my philosophy shifting? Why was I witnessing the scene instead of being part of it?

I haven't told too many people about the incident because I haven't sorted it out for myself. I have been hearing, though, of others experiencing the same phenomenon of being the observer. Those others are well-functioning, rational people who, like me, sometimes are literally beside themselves. We ask, *What am I meant to understand from this? Why am I eavesdropping on myself? What is it all about?*

We listen hard for the answers.

Bad Luck, Good Luck

The phone rang. It was my daughter calling from Italy to tell me not to worry, she was going to be late getting back to the States because her flight had been cancelled. The airline would put her up for the night. She bemoaned her bad luck. Her vacation was over and she wanted to be home.

Her complaint reminded me of an old Chinese story:

Once there was a poor farmer who lived with his son on a small farm. He had only one horse that he kept inside a weather-beaten fence.

One day, the horse ran away.

"What bad luck," said the neighbors.

"How do you know?" said the farmer.

The next day, the horse returned to the farm with several wild horses.

"What good luck!" said the neighbors.

"How do you know?" said the farmer.

As the farmer's son was training one of the horses, he fell off and broke his leg.

"What bad luck," the neighbors said.

"How do you know?" said the farmer.

When the soldiers came into the village, they took all the able-bodied young men to be in the army but they did not take the farmer's son because of his broken leg.

It seemed that my daughter was experiencing bad luck but then I told her that the airplane she had been scheduled on, TWA Flight 800, had exploded over the Atlantic on its way to Europe.

We both paused, she in Rome, I in New Jersey, before we thanked God for the wonderful good luck of a missed plane.

HEALING

HEALING

I cut my finger the other day. It wasn't a bad cut but enough to make me head for the aloe plant on my kitchen windowsill. I broke off a piece of the succulent, squeezed the leaf to release the liquid from the cells, slit it open with my fingernail, and applied the juice to the wound. The slimy substance was cold against my finger. It diluted the intense red to a light pink. As it dried, I added more until the bleeding stopped and the pain left. I thanked the plant for sharing its healing properties with me and went about my day.

My views on healing have changed in the last dozen years. I don't take antihistamines for my late summer allergy symptoms any more but use acupressure instead and save myself from the debilitating drowsiness and other side effects that used to be the price of relief. Two minutes of pressing yields hours of allergy-free activity. Colds, on the rare occasion I get them, also respond to acupressure as well as to herbs and homeopathy. Qi Gong and various other forms of eastern medicine, massage, imagery and meditative prayer help the assorted aches, pains, cramps, and discomforts of physical existence. I still see a medical doctor when necessary but not exclusively; I choose to approach my care through holistic means.

Holism attends to the whole of an organism rather than focusing on its parts. I know if I get sick, I was physically, emotionally, or mentally open to the bacteria or virus that found a friendly environment within my body. If I get rid of the illness but not the cause, I leave myself vulnerable to ailing again. I need to examine patterns I have created in my life, the thoughts that make illness acceptable. The pain in my leg is connected as much to the thought in my head as to its bodily irritation.

Sometimes, no matter what we do, we cannot be physically cured but that doesn't mean we cannot be healed. Healing is a broad concept. We may not be able to cure a damaged relationship but we can heal it. Shame cannot be cured but it longs to be healed. A person may heal a heart of hate and still experience a heart attack.

There are many groups that meet for the express purpose of healing. I participated in one where healing ourselves was seen not as a goal but as a process to greater global healing. We worked toward creating wholeness on all levels and supported each other's efforts in that direction.

What place has healing in a book about listening? Healing is a concept that is impossible without tuning into the universal information that comes to us. To receive that information, we have to listen. The notion of the teachable moment is based on it. We can hear something a hundred times in many different ways from an excellent teacher and not understand but when we are ready to listen, all we need is to hear it once from anyone at all and we will know it. If we want to heal our discomforts, it makes sense to listen to the messages those discomforts bring.

To heal the whole self, we must be willing to listen to all the information that comes through. Healing is an interactive process within ourselves because we are more complicated, more complete, than just a collection of parts.

Working Things Out

Claire's mother was back in the hospital. Another mitral valve needed replacing. Like an aging carburetor, her mother's heart was in the shop, yet again, for a new part.

The hospital was in Philadelphia, Claire lived in New York; I lived in between, just over the bridge. It was natural for Claire to stay with me while her mother was operated on. We were best friends. She would sleep here as her mother recuperated, then return to her home, family, and job. Meanwhile, we'd have a nice, long chance to talk without the inconvenience of a punitive monthly telephone bill.

Only her mother developed a fever and the doctors couldn't operate right away. Claire shuttled back and forth to the hospital for two weeks until she had to leave. She called her mother every day from New York. I called a few times but I did not visit. Hospitals made me uneasy so I stayed away. I didn't hear from Claire much but I knew she was busy and tired and involved with her mother's problems.

Then one day she called to tell me that her mother had died. She gave me the details of the funeral. I was surprised. I hadn't called that last week because I thought her mother had gone home. I felt sad that I hadn't done more but I had offered my house and meals and transportation and she had accepted.

I went to the funeral and gave what comfort I could. It was over; the many years of anxiety had come to an end. Claire cried on my shoulder. I held her close.

I was shocked when I received her letter a month later. I tossed it on the table as if it had exploded in my hand. It accused me of not fulfilling the duties of friendship by not tending to her mother in Claire's absence. She was disappointed. She was hurt. She had to write, she said, because if she didn't let me know how she felt, we could no longer be friends.

What had gone wrong? How could such good friends be so far apart?

I called immediately. We talked about how I didn't realize what she was really asking of me and how she had not communicated her expectations. We cried. My heart ached for her as well as with the pain I was feeling. We patched things up. For the time being. But this was a big wound that would need redressing.

Five years later, we talked about it again. This time she was apologetic. She said she was sorry that she sent that letter but that our friendship was too important to her to just let it drift away on unresolved hurts. I told her how grateful I was that she had. I learned more about how to be a friend because of that letter than from anything else.

Two years more passed before we finally laid the matter to rest. With a little perspective and a lot of forgiveness for our human failings both to communicate externally and to listen internally, we reclaimed the joy we shared in each other.

Healing Ourselves

For over a year, I met with seven people in a weekly healing group. We started without guidelines or structure and, while an informal format evolved, in some aspects it continued that way. We began by saying an opening prayer for light and clarity. We shared our experiences of the prior week in relation to the healing we had requested the last time. That was always great fun and it helped us to acknowledge universal responses. We asked for healing for ourselves, friends, family, the human family, the earth, whatever need we felt. We sat quietly. We said a closing prayer. What was said, who said it and how it was said was new, week-to-week.

We imposed no belief system on anyone. We came together – Unitarian, Catholic, Christian Scientist, Jew, Lutheran, practicing and non-practicing – for healing.

We took turns sharing any information that came to us out of our quiet sitting. It always made sense.

Slowly things changed. One member who was fearful became open and sunny. Another brought the same healing need time after time but lost her grayness and acquired a shine in her eyes. We reported that relationships with people around us were different, better, more peaceful. The earth seemed more hospitable, too.

It was a long drive for me to get to the meeting but I went in rain, in snow, when it was hot, when it was cold. How could I let such superficial things deter me from adding my voice and my prayers to a group that met for such a high purpose?

It was not a social group though the members certainly were sociable. No refreshments were served yet we all left refreshed. We were lighthearted but not trivial. We knew we had work to do. The work was not easy. We were in the process of healing our world through healing ourselves.

Qi Gong

When I practice Qi Gong, my hands come alive. The Chinese healing art, which means energy work, directs the flow of universal energy. The mere thought of using it sets my hands tingling with readiness, like a dog straining at the leash. My fingers become a dusty reddish-brown but within the center of my palms, there is a serene, white circle. It reminds me of an open door spilling out light.

As I prepare to work on my sister, even before I have focused on her, she says she feels a vibration coming from my hands. She used to think this was nonsense; now she asks me to help relieve the pain of foot surgery. She is attentive to the changes in energy flow when I direct the qi toward her.

My trainer at the gym is skeptical about energy work but he cannot deny, even though he doesn't understand, the heat he feels when I place my hands over the spot where he has strained his back. He says, whatever it is, his back feels better.

My friend says she gets low-grade electrical shocks when I work with her. Sometimes we can actually see the arc of the spark as the current jumps from one to the other.

People ask why I don't go into the field of professional healing. I say that I have a career already. I am just grateful to be able to help myself, my friends, my family. I happily share the knowledge I have because I know it doesn't belong to me. I tell them they can learn how to do what I do, too. I give them the name of my teacher but not many go.

Qi Gong comes from a folk tradition, passed down in families, and is quite practical. I use it to relieve headaches, dissipate stomachaches, renew flagging energy, lessen muscle strain. It is portable; it requires no equipment other than intention.

One day on a beach outing with a fair-skinned friend, the mosquitoes and sand flies were swarming all around. Because she was sensitive to chemicals and didn't want to use insect repellent, I taught her how to project her energy outward so the insects would leave her alone. They circled but never landed. Others were slapping themselves furiously but we were bug-free.

Once I cut my finger on a metal object. It was a painful gash. I was nowhere near medical aid or even a bandage so I cupped my hands around the finger for about twenty minutes. When I checked it again, the gash had closed and the wound looked about three days old, well on its way to healing. It was no longer painful.

This is a healing technique available to everyone. What people seem not to understand is that healing is a participatory activity. It is not something that is done to them but something that they help bring about. It might seem easier to go to a bottle for a pill than to focus the energy, but the pill may have undesirable effects while it temporarily relieves symptoms. As I, like my friend, am sensitive to chemicals and especially to medication, I find the natural ways of healing more compatible. And as I share qi work with others, they can choose to reclaim the responsibility for their own healing.

I look at the white circles forming in my palms and feel the familiar tingling as I write this. It is comforting to know that the energy is always at hand.

The Doctors vs. The Gods

June had cancer once. She had an operation. The tumor was removed. She was well. Then it came back. The doctors told her she must have another operation. June declined. They said she would die within the year if she didn't. She told them she would focus on living for the time she had left.

I called June, today. The telephone rang a long time before she picked it up.

"Did I wake you?" I asked. She usually dozed later in the day but perhaps she had taken an earlier nap.

"No," she said. "I was out planting pansies. Isn't it a gorgeous day?"

It has been two years since the doctors predicted her death. The cancer is growing and she tires easily but she finds life good. She had strengthened family relationships. She had come to understand true friendship. Each day brings the joy of what she calls *little things* that others might overlook.

She is realistic. She knows this is not a kind disease and it will make tremendous demands on her so she keeps herself as healthy as she can. She watches her nutrition. She rests when her body tells her to. When she is feeling strong enough, she stretches and does some gentle Yoga postures.

She also takes care of her inner needs. She reads. She meditates. She visualizes. Her outlook is generally positive. She entered a hospice program and surrounds herself with wonderful, helpful, uplifting people.

June is thinking of writing a letter to the oncologists who painted such a dire picture of her meager future. Her life is full, she says, richer than it has ever been. She wouldn't recommend this method of enhancing one's awareness but she has learned a great deal in this short period of time about living, about loving, about being human.

"The doctors don't know everything," she said. "I think that the gods just might have other ideas."

GIFTS

GIFTS

My parents never understood my attitude toward gifts. I liked to receive them but if I didn't, it was no big deal. I was pressured into having my only birthday party when I was nine years old. I was given a book, a game, and a puzzle that I kept for years until younger family members claimed them. I had a surprise Sweet Sixteen celebration because I wouldn't plan one for myself.

It wasn't that I had so much I couldn't use another thing. I had sufficient clothing to wear though my closet was not overburdened. I owned few toys but I had a lively imagination and preferred made-up games anyway. While my friends collected dolls, I had a collection of tiny plastic charms. Everyone collected comic books that were traded and borrowed and prized.

Part of my disinterest in receiving presents, no doubt, came from my shyness. Being the center of attention embarrassed me. I would feel the heat rise from my neck to stain my face a bright red. The discomfort of the embarrassment often overshadowed my enjoyment of the gift.

Then, too, I guess I just appreciated different kinds of gifts. I frequently slept at my cousin's house, which was special to me. My aunt made big family dinners for the big family I loved to be around. My cousin and I had adventures like running away from home until dinnertime and taking a train into the city all by ourselves. Another aunt gave me a hand-me-down bicycle, an old English racer that was much too high for me so that I couldn't sit and pedal at the same time, but I could go anywhere on that bike. The freedom I felt could not have been contained in a box.

As I grew older, I discovered that I liked to give gifts more than receive them. I had the joy of pleasing others with what I knew was the perfect gift. I gave my friends presents for no occasion and brushed aside their dismay when they had nothing for me.

The satisfaction I felt turned questionable, however, as I began to work on my spiritual awareness. What was my true motivation? Was I really being generous or was I trying to control my own discomfort? I saw that I was denying others the same joy of giving by my reluctance to receive. And if I shut myself off from the loving expressions of those close to me, then how could I accept the spiritual gifts I sought – peace, compassion, love? There would be no channel for them to come through.

I began to say "Thank you" to compliments without pushing them away or demeaning myself as unworthy of them. I didn't have to believe the words but I could accept the good wishes that prompted them. I smiled when someone presented me with an unanticipated gift without questioning my need for it. The intention behind the presentation was the true gift. But it was the shift in my viewpoint that became the most important gift of all.

My attitude toward receiving gifts is quite different now. Not only am I pleased to get them, I *expect* them. I expect, even before I open my eyes in the morning, that each day is a gift for me. Every moment is the gift of opportunity. A phone call is the gift of connection. I see that we are ultimately our own gift-givers and gift-getters. We receive in the fullest what we allow ourselves, through our perceptions, to gratefully accept.

A Handful of Dirt

Before Eric left for Israel, he asked if there was something he could get for me. The question was kind – Eric is my son's friend.

"Bring me dirt," I said.

"Dirt?" he asked.

"Yes, dirt."

"How much?" he wanted to know.

"Whatever feels right."

We joked about it. I was the only one who would ask for such a thing, he said, but he would try to get it.

Now he is home and he presented me with three gifts. The first gift is that even though I had asked for something so unusual, he had listened.

The second gift is that in the whirlwind of his activity, he remembered.

The third gift is that he took the time to fulfill my request and more.

I am holding a small bottle that contains earth from Jerusalem, sand from the Dead Sea, and stones from Masada. I will put it with the small collection of things I keep – a vial of sand from Australia's outback, a heart-shaped stone, a pinecone, and imperfect crystal, a tiny bird's egg, a button that states NEARSIGHTED VISIONARY – things that remind me of my inner travels rather than my worldly ones.

This is not just a souvenir from a country I have yet to visit but a special reminder that true gifts come in the most unexpected forms, sometimes even as a handful of dirt.

Powerful People

I consider myself really lucky to have friends who don't have a clue. They are not stupid. These are wise, talented, educated, effective women. They don't sit back passively and let the world take charge of their lives.

Jeannie says, "Trust in Allah but tie up your camel." So she prepares presentations that have made her the highest producing regional health representative in her company.

Sandra conducts spiritually based workshops in corporate settings where the participants are often hostile, resistant, and angry but they end up enthusiastically embracing a program to foster their highest good.

Anna Marie quietly walks into a room and it is hers. People of all ages seek her council with personal problems, moral angst, even mathematics; somehow they know she can help – and she does.

Dolores keeps an authoritarian establishment in check, whether it is a belligerent board of directors or an opinionated doctor, a teacher who hasn't thoroughly thought things through or a monsignor with an unenlightened viewpoint. Title or position doesn't impress her.

F.M. is birthing a television program single-handedly, from the idea's inception to the final camera work, all the while allowing it to grow organically.

They are powerful women. What makes them clueless is that their lives are unplanned. They aren't trapped by the illusion of the future. They allow each day, every minute, to unfold as it will. They don't have goals – but they have visions.

They envision work that is satisfying and creative, careers at which they succeed well. They envision relationships that are supportive, that bring out the best in them. They see their lives filled with abundance in all forms.

Their lives are not easy by conventional standards. Several of them are struggling financially. Chronic health problems are in the daily consciousness of others. Some are raising difficult children. The burdens of abuse and divorce are not unknown.

Yet, there is an inner sense of adventure, a knowing that underneath it all is an ordered chaos, a reason. They don't expect to know what it is nor does it matter. What has meaning is the journey and what they seek is the awareness that comes from being mindful of each step.

Blue Baby Blanket

I held a friend's toddler last night. He sat on my lap, his back resting on my chest. I felt waves of heat through my sweater. It reminded me of holding my own children and feeling that warmth against my heart. But my children are grown, my baby an adult. I felt a mixture of past delight and present longing and a strong welling up of love.

The boy turned his head without moving his body so that he was looking at me from a strange angle. I looked back, amused, and said something in that voice adults use to entice children to smile. He didn't smile, just continued to look. His clear eyes compelled mine. As I stared directly into them, I knew something inside me shifted, that I had softened somehow. We stayed like that for a longer time than I thought a two-year-old could possibly sustain. Then he wiggled out of my arms and went to where his sister was playing.

He came back almost immediately, walking with that stumbling toddler urgency, his left arm outstretched. In his hand was his blue baby blanket. He held it solemnly out to me. I reached out with my right arm and took it from him. "Thank you," I said in my most respectful adult voice, overwhelmed by his generosity and pre-verbal understanding. He smiled then, and without a word turned back to play.

Celebrating

Years ago, my husband and I received a gift bottle of champagne. We put it away for a special occasion, although we never defined what that might be.

The bottle moved with us from apartment to townhome to single house. Each move brought a new phase in our shared life but we were too busy packing and unpacking and adjusting to new spaces to set aside the time to celebrate.

The bottle saw the birth of two children but our friends and relatives arrived with baby gifts and wine. So we toasted with the new bottles and let our champagne age a little longer in its, by then, battered wooden case.

The bottle witnessed the opening of a business; the transition from being employee to being self-employed seemed so natural that we were well into it before we realized it was something to celebrate. We continued to save the champagne for something special.

Finally, the moment arrived – the signing of my first book contract. With great ceremony, my husband popped the cork as I stood, towel ready, to catch the expected rush of foam. Nothing happened. I tasted the precious golden liquid. It was flat and vinegary, the bubbles having escaped over two decades of living.

"We missed it," I said, a sense of regret mixed in with the disappointment.

My husband put his arm around me and said, "It looks like this champagne has been celebrating with us for years; we just didn't notice."

Leahe and the Angels

When the pain from leukemia grew too intense to bear alone, Leahe saw an angel. It didn't have a halo. There wasn't a face. No heavenly gown drifted about invisible feet. The room shimmered and took on a brightness where there was no lamp. She was eased by the presence.

When angina squeezed her chest so tightly she thought she would gladly have lost consciousness, Leahe felt an angel's hand on her shoulder. It was a large hand, heavy, not at all what she would have expected. But its weight comforted her until she could breathe again.

When despair shrouded her like a steel cocoon, Leahe heard an angel's song. It was so pure and beautiful, it lifted her from the grayness into a rainbow of sound.

When the sun rose from the sleeplessness of the blue night and hope stretched its elegant wings, Leahe talked to the creator of light and hands and music – and thanked God for the angels.

Meditating

Each morning, when the house is quiet, I ready myself for meditation. I take the telephone off the hook. I sit cross-legged and straight-backed on my sofa. I close my eyes.

At first I am aware of the sounds around me, sounds I did not hear as I moved about the house – a drizzle tapping at the drainpipe, the ticking of the clock, the chip of a cardinal. Then I gently draw my attention to my breathing and watch it settle down. I do not control it. When it assumes a natural, smooth, slow rhythm, I shift my attention to the space between my eyebrows, that space known as the third eye. I sense myself surrounded by white light; I connect with the light and wait.

Sometimes I just sit, focused on my breath. It relaxes me. I find the breath gets deeper and slower. If my mind starts to wander, I gently bring it back. I may have to refocus again and again but I do it without impatience because there is nothing else I need to be doing; I am just sitting and breathing.

Other times I focus on a concept such as love or compassion and allow whatever images or understandings I receive to play themselves out on my mind-screen. I don't question, I just receive.

I may ask the Universe for clarity about an issue that is bothering me or has me confused. I accept the information that comes through without analyzing it. There is plenty of time afterwards to mull it over.

Occasionally I ask for guidance for someone else. I may not understand the messages I get but then they aren't for me, so I just listen.

I have no sense of time when I meditate. What seems like three minutes may actually be twenty, five minutes can be half an hour or more. As I come back to the presence of the room, I slowly open my eyes and check my watch. I'm surprised again.

I replace the phone when I am ready to reconnect with the world. Only the world seems different. It has softer edges and brighter colors. It feels kinder and less frenetic. Maybe I am the one who exhibits these qualities but as the Universe and I are one, it doesn't matter.

Meditation is a gift I give to myself and, because of how I am changed, to the world. I wonder what the world would be like if everyone meditated every day.

UNDERSTANDING

UNDERSTANDING

I love the cartoon graphic of the lightbulb going on overhead when the character gets an idea. It seems so simple – an inner switch is flicked and understanding shines out. I wish I had a switch like that, one I could control. I need the solution to a problem? Flick, I have it! I'm confused about making a decision? Flick, the direction is clear. The answers to life's big questions elude me? Flick, not any more.

Opportunities for understanding are all around, yet I notice that much of the time my switch is turned off. I am blinded by what I expect to see. I look for a book in my bookcase that I am sure has a blue cover with red lettering and cannot find it even though I check and recheck the shelves. Did I lend it to someone? I wonder. As soon as I stop looking, the title pops out at me in the exact place I knew it would be, only the book has blue writing on a white background. By focusing on my pre-conceptions, I eliminate all possibilities but the one I expect and set myself up for failure.

As I search for truth, I sometime find myself doing the same thing. My idea of where it is to be found is so consuming, that I lose the peripheral vision that would help illuminate my quest. When I'm being particularly structured, a fog settles on my brain so that all new ideas are blocked. It becomes obvious then, that I need to back off, to relax my chokehold on truth as I know it or want it to be. I suggest to myself that I now see all possibilities clearly and that the solution I seek is within my understanding. Then I give myself permission to receive the knowledge. It seems to open the energy channels that eventually lead to the lightbulb, although I am usually surprised by the form it takes. The creative spirit is always brighter and more inventive than I anticipate.

For me, understanding mostly comes as a process. Whether I think about the topic at hand actively or go into receiver mode in meditation, I need to mull things over. Sometimes it feels plodding, like the seemingly endless stirring of the pudding until it thickens.

What I really seek is enlightenment, that shift from not knowing to knowing regardless of what is to be known. It is the instant of understanding before anything can be formed into words. It is the exhilaration of experiencing knowing on all levels with nothing apart, nothing separate.

And, once again, I see that I need to release a prior notion, that cherished cartoon image, for enlightenment is not the lightbulb but the switch.

Struggling With Truth

I had a boyfriend in high school who was creative,
humorous, and irreverent. I loved his company but I was
never totally comfortable with him. He was as creative
with the truth as he was with everything else.

We were in the same chemistry class. Chemistry was a
hard subject for me. I studied but my grades weren't great.
My boyfriend laughed.

"It isn't important," he said.

I studied anyway. When a test came up, I studied even
more.

The day of the midterm, I was a wreck. I looked around
for my boyfriend but he wasn't in class yet. The teacher
handed out the test papers. Where was he? He came in
late with his hand wrapped in a big, white bandage. A
bad sprain, he told the teacher, or maybe a hairline
fracture. He couldn't write. He was excused from the test.
He smiled at me as he left the room. Now I was worried
about him as well as passing the midterm.

I saw him in the lunchroom three periods later.

"How is your hand?" I asked.

He laughed his *Why study?* laugh.

"It's fine," he said. "See?"

The bandage was gone. He moved his hand around.
There was no sign of injury. He could see the confusion on
my face.

"I made it up," he said. "I didn't feel like studying.
Boy, are you gullible."

I guess I was. I believed what people said.

"How could you do that?" I asked.

"Look, I didn't really lie. I couldn't write because I didn't know the answers. I'll take the test another time when I'm ready. Gotta go."

I watched him take his tray back and head for the door. A group of kids surrounded him. I knew he was telling them about what he did. They were hooting.

I sat at the lunch table until the bell rang, thinking. To him, he wasn't really lying. To me, he wasn't telling the truth. He was happy. I was struggling.

The chemistry test came back a week later with a passing grade.

I stopped seeing my boyfriend.

San Clemente

Of all the churches in Rome, one of the most memorable is the church of San Clemente, on the banks of the Tiber River. It is small and simple, a modest building in a country known for its magnificent churches. It has a history, as does everything in Rome, and it is that history that lifts if from being just another church to an architectural metaphor.

When the Tiber is calm, it flows lazily between its high concrete banks; no one would suspect its majesty. But in the centuries before the embankments were constructed, Rome was at the mercy of this powerful river that periodically flooded its banks and buried parts of the city in mud. San Clemente is a witness to the process.

I visited San Clemente, one tourist among many, expecting to see the usual church features and, for the most part, there were no surprises. I saw statues and columns, cut glass windows dating from the fifteen hundreds. They were nice but not spectacular. Some people sat on the dark, wooden benches in prayer, others in weariness, as they must have from the time the church was built. It is a community church for everyday people. But this church holds a mystery of more than its saints and martyrs.

There is a small stairway almost hidden from view. I descended and discovered another church beneath the first! The statues here are different, less elaborate, and the artwork less familiar. This church dates from the eleven hundreds when the Tiber laid layer after layer of mud into it and it became unusable. The current church rests upon the remains of the older one.

I proceeded to another stairway, even harder to find, which leads further down. It is colder and earthier in this space. The statues are almost primitive. Niches here and there attest to altars and an active religious practice. Is it the cult of Mithras? There is no light coming in through the mud, no windows to penetrate the underground darkness. I put my hands against the cold earthen walls and felt the vibration of moving water. It is the Tiber rushing by, not so very far away. The river rules here.

Underneath is another space that hasn't been excavated because there isn't enough money to do it. The restorers know it is there and suspect there is at least one more level they say they may never see.

As I stood in the pulse of the river, it was tempting to go further, to want to dig into the inaccessible parts and uncover treasures from the mud. At the same time, it was frightening to be so entombed in the earth, not knowing what there was to be found.

As I came back up to the level of light, I felt as if I had been on an archeological dig within my psyche, each layer a deeper, darker, more primitive exploration of self. Yet what power was entombed there? Could it be tapped in a civilized way?

I left the tiny church to ponder the grand cathedrals whose interiors soar into the heights. It was comforting to be outside, to look upward and for a while forget that the many layers of San Clemente lie hidden within each of us.

House Robbers

I dreamed I heard robbers in my house. I walked down the stairs and found two men ripping up the wooden floor in my livingroom.

"What are you doing?" I asked. I was curious but not the least afraid.

"We're taking up the floorboards," one of the men replied.

"With all the electronic equipment and jewelry and things in the house, you want my floor?"

"We're not interested in that stuff. We want the hard, wooden boards," he said.

I watched for a while as he crowbarred the honey-colored slats.

He's ripping up my foundation, I thought.

Then, as if he could hear my thoughts, he looked at me sternly and said, "And when we finish with the floor, we're going to tear down your walls!"

I imagined what my house would look like with no floor and no walls. The frame was standing with glass-less windows and wood-free doors. I could see the sky through the missing structure. It was clear blue with white, billowy clouds gently floating by. Fresh air blew right through – I could feel the breeze brush my face. Birds flew into the house and out again, unimpeded. I sensed myself outside of my house at the same time I was inside.

The deep black of the earth cushioned my feet. I couldn't see through it but it vibrated through me, alive and pulsating. I felt I could slip down into it at any moment as easily as I could fly off into the sky. I had lost all my boundaries. How refreshingly strange it was.

The robbers were still busy with the floor. I heard the squeak of the boards as the nails let go their grip.

Hurry up, I thought. The walls are waiting.

Laughing

My yoga teacher laughed all the time. When I asked a question, he laughed. When I answered a question, he laughed. He laughed when he corrected me in a posture and sometimes he laughed, it seemed to me, at nothing at all.

When others in the class laughed with him, I assumed they all knew something I didn't. But I was a new student and self-conscious and could only imagine he was laughing at me. Perhaps I said something incredibly naïve or asked a really stupid question. Maybe my postures were executed so poorly there was nothing to do *but* laugh.

One day he laughed at my question and I suddenly had to know. I steeled myself and asked him why. Was my question so crazy? Were my concepts so lacking in understanding as to be laughable?

No, my question was a good one, he told me.

So why did he laugh?

When a person is connected with Universal Oneness, he said, no matter what happens, life is fun.

I knew many things in life that were definitely not fun. What he said made no sense to me but at least I was relieved that I was not the cause of his amusement.

I continued to practice Yoga. I read philosophy. I studied Eastern thought and Western religions. I employed holistic healing methods. I meditated.

And then one day, years later, I began laughing.

I laughed at getting sidetracked on the way to a meeting and then discovering the regular route was blocked.

I laughed when a book popped off the library shelf at me, the exact book I needed though I wasn't looking for it.

I laughed at noticing the same universal structure in the contents of a dumpster as there was in me.

I laughed in the middle of an argument.

I laughed at seeing the beauty of the headlights and taillights in a highway traffic jam.

I laughed to the baby in the shopping cart in front of me on the long supermarket line that wasn't moving.

I laughed over spilled milk.

I laughed with a friend for the shear joy of laughing.

I laughed because everything was an adventure and I was curious,

because one thing seemed to lead to another effortlessly,

because all things fit together in a puzzle I was just beginning to fathom.

I laughed for seven days and at the end of the week, my life returned to normal. Only, I was changed. It was as if I was back at that Yoga lesson a dozen years before and this time I understood.

The Living Artist

The article in the newspaper was about a memorial service and the unveiling of a statue for the six million Jews who were murdered in the Holocaust. An accompanying photograph showed stone flames rising in the air. The sculpture reminded me of a Holocaust seminar I had attended years ago.

I had volunteered to help. I was stationed at a table near the entrance to assist people in registering for the discussion groups in ethics, religion, law, human relations, history, and art. A tall, broad, thick-haired man studied the sign-up sheets. He picked one up and waved it in the air.

"Art? What kind of art?" he demanded.

"The drawings that came out of the concentration camps," I said.

His dark eyes glared at me.

"I came out of the concentration camps," he said. "The only art I saw was the art of survival."

He tossed down the paper.

"Look at me," he said. "I'm a living artist – I survived!"

He scrawled his name across one of the other sheets and walked off into the crowd.

When I went home, I looked up the word *art* in the dictionary. It was defined as "the production or expression of what is beautiful, appealing, or of more than ordinary significance." If staying alive in those horrific times wasn't beautiful, appealing, or of more than ordinary significance, I didn't know what was.

The statue was beautifully carved and poignant but the living artist helped me understand it was only one of the many art forms of the human spirit.

If Earl Were to Ask

Earl's face is a full moon beaming out its light. The light is mirrored in the faces of the people he meets who respond with smiles and softened lines.

He doesn't know it. He is worrying about the direction in which his life is going and can't see his radiance even when it is shining back at him.

Earl's laugh is a bird's song welcoming Spring. It is open and lively and draws others into it until all those around him find themselves laughing, too, and feeling good.

He doesn't hear it. He is drowning it out with inner doubts that sound like a crow's sharp caws peck, pecking at crumbs of self-esteem.

Earl's voice is a cello vibrating in its own rich depth. It is a mellow symphony of compassion as he comforts the men dying in the hospice he helped to found.

He doesn't feel it. He only knows the ache of indecision that keeps him from resonating with life's moments of joy.

If he were to ask me, I would tell Earl not to seek answers in the darkness but in the light, to listen to the call of the stillness within, to resound with the music of the Universe that echoes through him and through us all...if he were to ask.

Two On the Path

Erik Haines is a 4th degree, Black Belt Karate Master and poet. He has a class of students, although he doesn't consider himself a teacher. He shows them the physical moves that discipline the body and the mental exercises that discipline the mind.

His students love the kicks and the chops. Class after class they practice the bodywork that earns them the different colored belts. Their goal is the belt that Erik has held for years. It is the one that absorbs the light yet shines the least.

They work hard at earning the black belt so when they finally pass all the physical tests, they are baffled why Erik won't award it to them. He knows it is not enough. He waits for them to stop showing off. He is patient when they complain. He encourages them to help the others. When they least expect it, the belt becomes theirs. It is no longer a prize but a symbol. Then it shines from the inside out.

I do not teach because there is
nothing to teach.
I know this, therefore
I am called teacher.
You do not yet know this
so you are called student.
After much trial, effort and pain
you will find written
on the page of self
I already know
what I have tried so
hard to learn!
This is called discovery.

Armed with this discovery
you will see that there was
nothing to learn.
This is called knowledge.

How can there be a teacher
or a student
if there is nothing to teach
and nothing to learn?

Only two on the path.

This is called understanding.

Erik Haines

RECONSTRUCTION

RECONSTRUCTION

My father is a multi-talented man. He can draw. He does calligraphy. He caters large parties and turns melons into sculptures to decorate the grand tables. He knows his way around a toolbox and is a general fix-it kind of guy.

Growing up, I liked watching him do whatever he was involved in but I especially loved when he let me help with his remodeling projects. I held the end of the board he was sawing so the wood would not snap off and splinter. I scraped off wallpaper, sanded plaster, brushed on paint.

He once built a diningroom from scratch. He tore down walls and put them up again somewhere else. He trimmed the room in molding and finished it off with the application of red, tartan wallpaper. He did it in his spare time after and around his three jobs, providing me with a course in spackling and weeks of chalk from the scraps of plasterboard he cut away. His friends and the neighbors marveled at the almost sudden appearance of this new room, literally created from thin air.

When the chalk and the newness were gone, I stopped thinking about the way the house had once appeared, as if this space had always been there. What never left me, though, was the feeling that walls were not permanent. I could look beyond them. A little destruction didn't frighten me for I knew, because I was part of it, that creation was following close behind.

As an adult, I have come to realize that there are more challenging reconstruction projects than rearranging physical walls. Inner reconstruction can be shattering and there are no blueprints to guide us. The only rule that seems applicable is that we are never too young or too old to create new spaces for ourselves.

And that is the interesting part of living – the rearranging, reconstructing, reconfiguring that goes on constantly on what outwardly appears to be a limited area. A change in one section alters the energy of the whole. When something in our thought pattern blocks our development, we can remember that it is only a wall that has been constructed and can be removed.

We are all interior designers making our emotional, mental and spiritual houses reflect our advancement. It requires choices, to be sure, often ones that set us apart from those around us. We may not always be clear as to what is happening, which is what listening is all about; it helps us to know when it is time to gather our tools and rebuild.

Turkish Taffy

When I was a kid, I used to love Turkish Taffy candy. Not only was it intensely sweet but it lasted all day. I would carry it in my pocket and gnaw off bites like a baseball player working a plug of tobacco. The wrapper got a little sticky from my saliva but it didn't matter. I could always leave it open until it dried. By then, of course, the taffy would have stuck to the paper and had to be pried off which made a most satisfying sound, especially in a silent classroom.

Turkish Taffy was best frozen. I would put it in the freezer overnight. Then, before opening it, I'd wham it against the Formica kitchen table. If my mother, who hated the noise, caught me first, she would shoo me outside and I would slam it down on the concrete steps out front. The taffy shattered into different sized pieces, some the right size for sucking on right away (they were still too hard to chew) while others were good for re-wrapping and saving for later in my back pocket. The candy would eventually thaw and become incredibly gooey which made it even more fun. The broken pieces were always plentiful which was a good thing because with Turkish Taffy, there were always friends around.

But, had I an endless supply of taffy to shatter, I would have given it all away; it was the shattering that most excited me. There was something intriguing about the squares and triangles, bits and pieces, dribs and drabs that were perfectly outlined in the wrapper. Each smashed bar was the same size and shape outside but different inside. Sometimes I would move the pieces around and then try to put them back together again. They never fit the same way as before, no matter how much I worked at it. I wondered why, if the pieces were all there, how come they only fit one way.

I haven't had Turkish Taffy for years yet I was reminded of it recently when, during a philosophical discussion, something was said that smashed me to bits. It was a simple statement, that truth was not a stopping point but an arrow indicating a direction. I felt my whole body physically shift although I was absolutely still in my chair. My familiar thoughts found new pathways. My frame of reference was no longer there.

I tried to reconfigure myself but couldn't fit into the old shape. I found myself crying, although I wasn't sad. I knew I was grieving for what had been and would never be again. It was as if some giant cosmic hand had whammed my inner self against an invisible table.

I am still rearranging the pieces.

The Kindness of the Universe

"What does this dream mean, Mom?" my son, Russell, asked when he was sixteen.

The dream showed him walking through a formal garden that had Greek statues all around. Only the garden was not the serene place it was meant to be. The flowerbeds were filled with weeds. The paths were in disarray. The once grand marble statues were cracked and surrounded by crumbling stone walls.

Knowing that dream images are symbolic and refer to some aspect of the dreamer, I tried to be open to the language the dream was speaking.

"Well, with the classical images all falling to pieces, I think it is showing you a picture of something traditional in your life that is breaking apart," I said. "The things you have been counting on, your foundations, are changing."

"Why are the statues smashed? Parts of their bodies are broken and some have cracked heads."

"I don't know, Russ. The ancient Greeks were an intellectual people. Maybe there will be a break in the way you think about things now."

We couldn't imagine at the time what might change in his young life that would shatter such a garden.

The next week Russell was diagnosed with diabetes.

And diabetes does change the way in which a person exists in the world. The very foundation of physical existence depends upon how the body processes what we eat. With this disease, the pancreas no longer produces the insulin that ushers the nutrients into the cells. A person eats and drinks prodigious amounts and starves.

Insulin must be injected into the body manually to replace its loss. But too much insulin can send the body into shock and coma. The person with diabetes walks a tightrope of finding the correct amount to inject. That requires drawing a drop of blood several times a day to monitor the blood sugar level which is affected by many things – food, exercise, illness, stress.

It is hard to maintain a sense of wholeness and serenity when you are the one responsible for keeping yourself alive. The boundary of your body's safety, the symbolic garden wall, has crumbled. Just as in Russell's dream.

My son spent a week in the hospital learning how to think in new ways about what to eat, when to eat, how to exercise. He practiced the mechanics of monitoring and injecting himself under the watchful eyes of the nurses. We talked a lot during that time. One of the things we talked about was his dream. Was it prophecy? Was it a warning?

I see the dream more as a kindness, a compassionate message sent by his higher self. It was preparing him for a shattering experience. And because he shared it with me, I, too, was being prepared.

Never Say Never

When I first became vegetarian, my mother cried. She thought I was going to die. She pleaded with me to eat a little chicken, some fish. She was at a loss for what to serve me when I came to dinner although I stuffed myself silly on the abundant vegetables she always placed on the table.

My brother-in-law offered me five thousand dollars to eat a hamburger. I don't know what he would have done had I accepted but I thanked him politely and declined. I was invited to meals at expensive steakhouses and other bribes from assorted well-meaning relatives and concerned friends. Thanks, but no, I said.

People tried to argue me into eating meat. My motives and morals were questioned because I wore leather shoes, as if by catching me in an inconsistency my whole value system would collapse. I used to get angry and argue back until I recognized the pattern. Somehow, it seemed to me, if I were to eat meat, their dietary choices would be validated. So I stopped arguing. I just told them it didn't matter what they said, I would never eat meat again.

For over twenty years I happily ate only grains, vegetables, and fruit. Everyone got used to my eating regimen and left me alone. My mother stopped worrying. In fact, she stopped cooking altogether. When we shared a meal, it was at a restaurant so I could order whatever I wanted without her feeling guilty. My brother-in-law still tried to get me to "slip" but he did not extend bribes any more. At catered affairs, my meal was usually the most appealing. Only the occasional boor argued as vegetarianism became acceptable in society. I became acceptable.

Then I received a message while meditating that I was to start eating fish. It was not a welcome message. I tried to squirm out of it, telling myself that I was making it up, knowing that I wasn't. I was given specific instructions: I was to eat fish up to three times a week with three being optimal. I was to eat only white fish or salmon but no seafood. I was still not to eat meat or poultry.

I tried bargaining. What if I eat blue-green algae? That has all the nutrients I need. Fine, came the answer, eat algae – and fish. It is not only physically that the fish will be of benefit but on all levels. Do I have to? No, you always have the choice.

This was where my motives and morals stood on the line. Did I believe in listening, truly believe? Yes. Have I ever been given false or detrimental information? No. Did I always understand the information I received at the time? No. Was I so deeply attached to my self-definition of vegetarian that I was willing to negate the message? Maybe. No.

It took two weeks before I could buy a small salmon fillet. I prepared it in as loving a way as I knew how and ate three ounces. The once familiar texture was strange in my mouth. The taste was good, I suppose, but not a factor. Twenty minutes after I ate it, I was aware that there was something foreign in my body. The awareness lasted a couple of hours.

Is it still in my highest interest to eat fish? I questioned. Yes.

The next week I ate flounder. Again, the strangeness and the awareness – and the affirmation that it is to my benefit to eat fish. So I continue to eat it and keep on questioning.

In time, I expect the physical discomfort will leave me. What may take some work is the mental uneasiness, not because I am eating another living being for plants are living, too, but because for so long I was calling myself vegetarian and now I cannot honestly say that I am. I suspect that is part of this awareness. I was as attached to the label as I was to the philosophy that drew me to it.

People have begun to tease me again.

"You eating fish?" said a friend. "This I have to see."

"I finally got used to your crazy eating habits and now you go and change them," my husband complained.

So far, no one has offered me money though I wouldn't be surprised if the arguments about my morals start up anew. I can hear them now: Killing fish is as bad as killing an animal so why won't you eat meat? You said you would never eat meat, fish, or poultry again, remember?

My own words arguing against me. I had not realized how confining a small word such as *never* could be. Only I won't argue. This isn't about food, after all. It's about listening and connectedness and maybe even about courage – the courage to let go of a definition in order to more clearly define myself.

Making Movies

My first memory is of being lost. I was three years old.
I wanted to play with my sister and her friends who were
double my age. They didn't want me around but I kept
following them. They ran away, down the block. I hurried
as fast as I could after them. They turned the corner. I was
there, a step or two or three behind. Okay, they said. You
can play. They led me into a courtyard and told me we
were going to play Hide and Seek. I was It. I had to close
my eyes and count to ten – verrry slowly. I was proud of
my newly learned counting skills, so I began. One. Two.
Three...

When I opened my eyes, they were gone. I looked
around the courtyard. The apartment houses loomed like
towers even though they were only two stories high. I
knew I would never find my sister and her friends but I
wasn't concerned with that any more. How would I ever
get home? My mother didn't know where I was.

I had the image of night coming and there I would be,
wandering in the dark, cold and hungry. It did not matter
that it was mid-morning and summer. I felt the chill.

The brown buildings turned gray. The chirping birds
faded from hearing. The flowers in the flowerpots and the
bright laundry dancing on thick clotheslines from kitchen
windows became colorless. I no longer felt part of the
world. My surroundings closed in on me and I cried with
the certainty that I was as alone as if I was the last person
on earth.

A gentle hand reached out with a handkerchief. I had
not seen the old man approach. He seemed familiar yet I
couldn't quite remember who he was.

"Are you lost," he asked.

I nodded.

"Aren't you Sam and Shirley's daughter?"

Another soggy nod.

"I'll take you home."

He put out his hand and I took it, a lifeline to physical reality. As we walked slowly out of the courtyard, colors returned. We turned left at the corner and I recognized the big street I wasn't allowed to cross by myself. Another left and the block, *my* block, hummed with life. I felt reborn. The feet in the tiny white and brown saddle shoes were *my* feet. The hand holding tightly to Grandpa Garelick's hand (I suddenly remembered, he was one of my parent's friends) was *my* hand. This was *my* house we were going into, *my* stairs, *my* door, *my* life.

My parents laughed in surprise when Grandpa Garelick showed up with me clinging to him.

"You were only around the corner," they said.

But I didn't know it.

"What a baby," my sister whispered in my ear.

Well, I was. Chronologically. But I grew up that day in a way I did not yet understand. I learned how perception creates reality, how the inner state programs what is seen in the outer world much as a movie reel projects pictures on a screen. And just now, as I write this, an adult far from babyhood chronologically, do I accept that I am the producer of my own movies.

LISTENING WITH ELOISE

Eloise, my pet cockatiel, laid an egg today. She laid it on the metal grid that separates the upper cage from the removable plastic bottom. There was no nesting box, no feathery down to cushion its arrival – a no-frills birth. When she was finished, Eloise left the perfect white egg and climbed out the door and up the bars to the top of the cage. Then she looked at it curiously from her new perspective as if to ask, What is that? Did I create it? Her ruffled feathers betrayed her bewildered state.

I laughed at her bewilderment because I knew exactly what she was feeling. When I send a book off to my publisher, I become detached from it. The effort that brought it to completion is remembered in a disconnected way, a momentary burden left behind. It comes back bound and beautiful. I stare at it, like Eloise stared at her egg. Did I create that? I wonder.

My grown children visit me, bringing their new poise and confidence. They share the lives they are fashioning for themselves out of the childhood rules, bedtime stories, genetic inheritance, Thanksgiving dinners, friendships old and new. It is hard not to stare in amazement at these glorious creations. Where did they come from, anyway?

This process of creation amazes me. Oh, I understand how babies, human and otherwise, are made. I give talks on how books are born, even how to get the ideas that spark the books. It is the concept of the idea that is so fascinating. First, there is nothing, then this new something. Is every idea a birth? Is every birth, whether physical, emotional or mental, the response to an inner dialogue?

What did Eloise hear when she presented the world with the egg? Perhaps it was only instinct but isn't that a dialogue between inner urge and outer reply? This book came into being because an idea took life in my mind and in my heart; I had to acknowledge it in some way. There is a dynamic interplay between the listening and the response and then the echo that provides opportunity for further listening.

Eloise had listened and responded. I praised her for the lovely egg she produced.

There was comfort in realizing that the two of us were part of the same larger picture, that everyone, all of creation, had inner access to universal knowledge. We could know the answers to the mysteries of the Universe through our own, personal listening.

Eloise relaxed and fluffed her feathers. We snuggled, beak to cheek, spiritual companions on the continuing journey.

About the Author

Ferida Wolff has been exploring the inner terrain of the self for thirty years. She has taught Yoga to children and adults and leads workshops to introduce people to the process of listening.

Ms. Wolff studies Kabbalah and Buddhism. She practices Qi Gong, Tai Chi, Ayurveda, Acupressure, Applied Kinesiology, and Therapeutic Touch. She has been initiated into first degree Reiki and holds certificates in Foot Reflexology and Holistics Studies. She has a Master of Science in Education from Queens College.

Ms. Wolff combines her holistic knowledge with her writing. She has published fourteen books for children, many on themes that encourage new ways of looking at one's surroundings and observing the self. Her articles for newspapers and magazines range from the arts to *zazen*.

Order Form

LISTENING OUTSIDE LISTENING INSIDE

Thank you for your interest in Universal Vision books. For additional copies of LISTENING OUTSIDE LISTENING INSIDE by Ferida Wolff (ISBN 0-9671540-0-6), please use this form. For more information about Universal Vision, visit our website at WWW.Univ-Vision.Com.

Number of Copies Ordered _____ @ $15.99 each $_____.____
Less 5% Volume Discount (10 or more books)   -_____.____
Subtotal $_____.____
Add 6% if NJ Resident   +_____.____
Postage and Handling: First Book   +___ 3. 50
$2.00 each additional book to same address   +_____.____
Total Amount Due: $ _____.____

Form of Payment:
( ) Enclosed is my check (or money order) payable to
    Universal Vision
( ) Please charge my account   ( ) Master Card ( ) Visa
    Credit Card Number _____Exp. Date____
    Name of Cardholder_____
    Signature of Cardholder_____

Send to:
Name_____
Address_____State_____Zip_____
Phone Number (Day)_____ (Evening)_____

PLEASE RETURN THIS FORM WITH PAYMENT TO:
UNIVERSAL VISION, P.O. BOX 2350, CHERRY HILL, NJ 08034-0186

To order another essential book from Universal Vision, please turn to the other side.

Order Form

CO-CREATING ONENESS

Another book of interest from Universal Vision, CO-CREATING ONENESS by Sandra C. Brossman (ISBN #0-9671540-1- 4), uncovers the spiritual meaning underlying society's current turmoil. It empowers readers to create a life based on inner spiritual values through a process of emotional healing and reveals how we can focus our energy to manifest a reality of inner peace and universal harmony.

Number of Copies Ordered _____ @ $20.99 each $_____.___

Less 5% Volume Discount (10 or more books)   -_____.___

Subtotal $_____.___

Add 6% if NJ Resident   +_____.___

Postage and Handling: First Book   +___3. 50

$2.00 each additional book to same address   +_____.__

Total Amount Due: $_____.__

Form of Payment:

( ) Enclosed is my check (or money order) payable to Universal Vision

( ) Please charge my account   ( ) Master Card ( ) Visa

Credit Card Number _____Exp. Date____

Name of Cardholder_____

Signature of Cardholder_____

Send to:

Name_____

Address_____State_____Zip_____

Phone Number (Day)_____ (Evening)_____

PLEASE RETURN THIS FORM WITH PAYMENT TO:
UNIVERSAL VISION, P.O. BOX 2350, CHERRY HILL, NJ 08034-0186